Baseball

The Secrets & Techniques That Will Help You Make the Team and How the System Works

(Everything Young Readers Need to Know About the Baseball)

Andre Daly

Published By **Simon Dough**

Andre Daly

All Rights Reserved

Baseball: The Secrets & Techniques That Will Help You Make the Team and How the System Works (Everything Young Readers Need to Know About the Baseball)

ISBN 978-1-7771462-1-4

No part of this guidebook shall be reproduced in any form without permission in writing from the publisher except in the case of brief quotations embodied in critical articles or reviews.

Legal & Disclaimer

The information contained in this book is not designed to replace or take the place of any form of medicine or professional medical advice. The information in this book has been provided for educational & entertainment purposes only.

The information contained in this book has been compiled from sources deemed reliable, and it is accurate to the best of the Author's knowledge; however, the Author cannot guarantee its accuracy and validity and cannot be held liable for any errors or omissions. Changes are periodically made to this book. You must consult your doctor or get professional medical advice before using any of the suggested remedies, techniques, or information in this book.

Upon using the information contained in this book, you agree to hold harmless the Author from and against any damages, costs, and expenses, including any legal fees potentially resulting from the application of any of the information provided by this guide. This disclaimer applies to any damages or injury caused by the use and application, whether directly or indirectly, of any advice or information presented, whether for breach of contract, tort, negligence, personal injury, criminal intent, or under any other cause of action.

You agree to accept all risks of using the information presented inside this book. You need to consult a professional medical practitioner in order to ensure you are both able and healthy enough to participate in this program.

Table Of Contents

Chapter 1: The History Of Baseball From The 19th Century Until Today 1

Chapter 2: Modern-Day Baseball 14

Chapter 3: The Role Of Tv And Social Media 21

Chapter 4: Video Games Featuring Baseball 28

Chapter 5: Locations And Small Markets 42

Chapter 6: International Leagues 57

Chapter 7: Confusion Baseball With Softball.. 71

Chapter 8: International Stadiums 85

Chapter 9: What Can You Do To Increase The Popularity Of Baseball? 98

Chapter 10: What Is Baseball? 143

Chapter 1: The History Of Baseball From The 19th Century Until Today

Baseball's creation is perhaps the most distinctive invention of a game.

Alexander Cartwright is considered one of the founding fathers of baseball. While Abner Doubleday is often considered to be the first person to invent baseball however It is Alexander Cartwright who designed the first rules for baseball, though the significance of his contribution in the evolution of the game is debated. The first time players played the game, they threw their ball underhand rather than throwing the ball overhand. It was a lot like softball. It was not a sport played by gloves and the fence around outfields was not in place and at that time, there was no deck circle. In the United States it was a gradual growth of the game until, by the end of 1800 it became a most popular pastime.

The very first professional league for baseball was called The National League of Baseball. The league was established on February 2nd of 1876, by an Chicago businessman called William Hulbert. In 1869, The Cincinnati Red Stockings became America's first professional baseball team. They are now called "the" Cincinnati Reds.

It was 1903 when Major League Baseball had its first World Series. It was the Boston Red Sox, who at the time were known by the name of Boston Americans, defeated the Pittsburgh Pirates in a 4-2 series victory. The game was easy back in the day. There wasn't a designated hitter nor switching hitting. Every player had to get up onto the field and strike. Two of the best teams in the American League and National league could play for the World Series and that was the end of it. There wasn't a wild card game or playoffs. You needed to be at the top or else you wouldn't have the chance to participate part of the World Series.

The game continued to progress and grew, switch-hitting as well as pinch-hitting became a reality. At first, the batter had the option of choosing how the ball he was going to hit, and which was either on the left side or on the right side. Pinching was the next thing to happen. If a team is down by a few points or needed their favorite player for a specific time, they can get the player. With using the double switch the pitcher could be used as a substitute for a batter, while a fielder is substituted and put at the same time.

Expansion and Realignment:

New York, Chicago, St. Louis, and Boston were once the major hubs of baseball. The four cities featured at least two teams from the 1950s onwards These were the four cities where baseball was cherished the most. There was a period when there wasn't any professional sports team west beyond St. Louis. California baseball didn't really begin to gain traction until. It was not until 1957 that the New York Giants and Brooklyn Dodgers made their way towards San Francisco and Los Angeles and Los Angeles, respectively. Growing popularity of baseball created a desire for more professional teams. Teams like those of the LA Angels and New York Mets began their inaugural seasons in 1961 and 1962, and played in the same cities as Dodgers as well as the Yankees.

In the year 1961, Minneapolis would receive the first professional baseball team. It is now referred to under the name Minnesota Twins. The initial Washington Senators would move to Minneapolis as well. Washington D.C. would get an expansion team which was dubbed"the" Washington Senators.

The St. Louis Browns moved to Baltimore in 1954. They later changed their name to known as the Baltimore Orioles. In 1954 in 1954, they were also the Philadelphia Athletics moved to Kansas City. Then, in 1968, they relocated to Oakland and are there currently.

In 1969, four additional MLB teams joined the league. These were the

San Diego Padres, the Kansas City Royals, the Seattle Pilots and the Montreal Expos (known now under the name of Washington Nationals). They Expos are the very first official Canadian sports team. They were followed by the Toronto Blue Jays would join the league in 1977, becoming their second official Canadian baseball team.

Expanding and realigning was the best time to do it. It allowed baseball to enter new areas, and grew the MLB fan base. California baseball is perhaps the most crucial aspect of the adjustment and expansion. Since baseball teams like the Dodgers and Giants arriving in LA in addition to San Francisco respectively, growing cities had new baseball teams to support for. With the expansion of teams into the league, MLB started to generate more money and increase the number of fans it had.

Baseball is coming from the south.

The Houston Astros were the first major expansion team from the south region in the United States. They also were Houston's first professional team. The team was initially named"the Colt 0.45s in 1962, they later change their names to the Astros in the month of December during the season of 1966. They began in 1966 to play at the Astrodome. They would be the Houston Astros would be the first professional baseball team in the world to play indoors at a dome stadium. They would use artificial turf that was appropriately dubbed Astroturf. It was the time that the Milwaukee Braves came to Atlanta in the year 1966. In 1966, the Braves were the very first major league team to make the move into the Southeast. Since there were no Major League teams in the Southeast the need for baseball increased.

1970s Relocations:

It was reported that the Washington Senators would play their final game at Robert F. Kennedy (RFK) Stadium on September 30th 2001. Following the season of 1971, they Washington Senators moved to Arlington, Texas and became the Texas Rangers. The Rangers were only the 2nd team from Major League Baseball that came to Texas.

In 1969 in 1969, the Seattle Pilots had their first game in Seattle. It was also their first MLB team from the Northwest The owner of the team, Dewey Soriano, refused to finance the team. So he transferred the team to Bud Selig, who had considered bringing the sport back to Milwaukee. After the sale was completed it was renamed The Milwaukee Brewers and began their debut season in the year 1970. Seattle was to receive a second baseball team. It was the Seattle Mariners would begin their debut season in 1977.

The playoffs are being restructured:

At the time that MLB was created for the first time when it was first created, the top American League team and the top National league team could compete at the World Series. The structure was in place till 1968, and it continued even after the MLB was expanded to include 20 teams.

In 1969, the MLB was expanded to include 24 teams. Each league was divided into two divisions: Eastern or Western. The MLB extended the playoffs during the season of 1969 and introduced an entirely new round of playoffs, called"The League Championship Series (LCS) which is a best-of-five-series. In 1985, the LCS was extended to seven games.

The 28 MLB teams modified their division structures. At first it was the case that each of the American League and National League included divisions of East division and a West. In 1994, the MLB created an additional Central division for both the American League and the National League as well as changed the structure of playoffs. The MLB also added a wild card playoff slot for the divisional winner from both AL and NL who had the highest overall record, and also created the Division Series round. The wild card team took on Division winner who had the highest results in a best-of five-game series, while the two division winners competed against each other in a game that was best of five. The top two teams from each Division Series then played each the other in a best-of seven Championship Series with the winner winning play in the World Series. Due to the 1994 player strike The new format of playoffs could not be implemented until 1995.

In 2012 it was the year that the MLB introduced another wild card slot to the team that is not a division winner and has the second highest performance. The two teams with wild cards competed in a game of play-in and the winner advanced into the Division Series against the division winner who had the highest performance for the year. The play-in game gives teams more of the chance to make it to the World Series and adds to the excitement that comes with this year's MLB playoffs.

1990s Expansion:

In 1993, the Colorado Rockies and the Florida Marlins were added to in 1993 with MLB in 1993 as teams that were expanded. In 1993, the Florida Marlins would play in the same stadium with the Miami Dolphins. It was the first time it was the first time that Miami and Denver could each play host to the same MLB team. The year 1998 saw two more expansion teams were added to the league. These comprised The Arizona Diamondbacks and the Tampa Bay Devil Rays. These two teams were the final expansion teams of the MLB.

The Steroid Era:

Barry Bonds, Mark McGuire and Sammy Sosa were three of the top home run batters of all baseball from the beginning to mid-1990s. Mark McGuire and Sammy Sosa hit upwards of 50 home runs in consecutive seasons. In the 1990s and into the 2000s, everybody who had a passion for baseball was aware of the three men.

What they didn't understand initially was that they were suspected of using steroids, as were many others. They enjoyed a tremendous advantage in their time at the plate. One thing that did help pitchers was that players who went to the plate had to determine what pitches they would choose to throw.

The issue of steroids became to be so controversial, Congress became involved. Participants had to be questioned by the lawmakers the extent to which they had taken steroids. A few of them, like Rafael Palmiero lied under oath on the subject of not using steroids.

Chapter 2: Modern-Day Baseball

The evolution of baseball was distinct from the early 19th century design.

What has been changed include the rules, uniforms, as well as the design of stadiums. The stadiums are not as attractive as the sport from the time the game first began. There have been many positive advancements to the game through many years, such as the designated batter. A different rule has included the capability to contest specific play.

The introduction of the designated hitter was meant to alter those in the American as well as the National League. In reality, it was just those in the American League got the rule changes. In 1973 The American League played their first season using designated hitter rules. American League teams didn't have to be concerned about their pitchers stepping up to bat, and becoming a simple out. They could instead include a power-hitting player in their lineup and also keep pitchers from the batting order. It is the National League however, almost did adopt this policy. It's funny they were just one vote short of making this policy in place between the two leagues. What makes designated hitters an effective rule is that it allows players playing with no need to go out on the field. This means that the pitcher is able to concentrate on pitching.

A few people consider this a bad policy, since some think that pitchers shouldn't be given an advantage just because he throws the ball the best. Furthermore, the major league pitchers have proved their ability to hit the ball well over the years. Pitchers like Madison Bumgardner and Daniel Hudson have shown themselves to be capable of achieving decent average batting scores, despite being in the toughest field position.

Perhaps the greatest improvements to be made for Major League Baseball is managers being able to challenge specific decisions. In the past the teams were unable to argue or dispute any ruling. What the umpire declared was final and the coaches and players must accept the decision. The manager now has the right to appeal two times in a game, provided that the first challenge results in the decision to overturn it. Managers don't need to be concerned about losing an opportunity to timeout since they are unlimited in the game of baseball. Umpires are also able to step in to review home run call calls at any time during the game.

The delay and cancellation of World Series seasons:

There's been numerous seasons of lockouts in the NHL, NFL, and NBA. The MLB has not been an the only one to be affected by this. There was the absence of a World Series for the MLB. Also in 1994, there was the absence of a World Series. It also delayed the season of 1995. Although professional baseball has played for more than 100 years, but it has its own problems when it comes down to the playing of seasons.

In 1904 In 1904, in 1904, the New York Giants won the National League title. However, the American League title would come up for grabs between two teams: the Boston Americans and the New York Highlanders. The Boston Americans were the winners of their American League title. However, the

New York Giants, however did not want to join with the Boston Americans. The Giants protested at the fact that their main competitors and their rivals, the New York Highlanders were leading in the American League, but lost the title to Boston. There is speculation there was a conspiracy by the American League manipulated the results from the three previous matches to ensure that the two New York teams wouldn't play against each against each other.

1994 was the following season without the World Series. In 1994 the players' union was on strike. The major issue surrounding the strike was the cap on salary. It was clear that players were losing money as once players reached an amount, it could not make it easier for a top player who was earning more. The strike was unavoidable. The 1995 season didn't start until the 25th of April. Three weeks of the season weren't played in that season. However, the MLB held the World Series, which the Atlanta Braves won.

Some people believe baseball to be the best game ever played:

A majority of Americans have played in or watched a baseball game during their lives. Many believe that it is the most enjoyable game ever. The best part of baseball is that any player is a hero in any circumstance in any moment. In the event that a hitter who has poor batting skills is able to make an appearance at the plate when the bases are full and the team has lost by three runs, the hitter can take the lead with just one strike. Baseball is the one sport that an average player can take part in the game, and eventually become an international star. It doesn't require you to be a super athlete or tall in order to be a star. All you need is an athlete who is willing to study and put in the effort each day, when you head to the ballpark.

Chapter 3: The Role Of Tv And Social Media

Nowadays, on social media it is common to see news about sports focused on football or basketball while hockey has been slowly making momentum. Baseball is an entirely different thing. If you look on the top of the list on Twitter You'll be surprised when you discover anything related to baseball. There are many different sites to publish baseball related video content. What makes social media different from television is the fact the fact that it allows for discussions on any topic and view any video at any time you'd like to.

Instagram:

One might think that a social network which thrives on pictures and videos of short length could be the best place to highlight highlights of great plays and home runs. You'd be wrong, but the MLB typically gets overshadowed with NBA or NFL highlights. A single home run from Bryce Harper or Aaron Judge isn't as thrilling in the form of a slam-dunk highlight. Most of the time in basketball, it is more exciting and action-packed, while baseball's comes with a flurry of. Many kids are bored having to wait just a short time after each match to catch what happened and not having a constant movement and just relying on the clocks to stop play.

YouTube:

The majority of people do not need cables to stream their favourite sporting events. YouTube TV is a great option. YouTube TV, you can register and enjoy every professional sport league at an incredibly low cost. There are often no-cost games that are broadcast via YouTube TV. MLB YouTube channel.

YouTube is the ideal platform to stream baseball-related videos. Any type of sport you'd like to see you will find it on YouTube. For instance, if you are looking to understand how improve your performance in shortstop, you could look at instructional videos for beginner as well as advanced players. You may also see playlists of workouts specifically for the position that you would like to master. This can be useful for those who want to know the latest tips and techniques during the process.

Jimmy O'Brien, better known as "Jomboy Media is a YouTube sports commentator who reviews highlights of the baseball game and also other sports. The commentator often makes jokes or gets deep into the play and explains what transpired in that particular game. Viewers on YouTube can have fun while learning things they have never before. It helps to grow the sport since there's an element of comedy alongside baseball.

It is the MLB YouTube channel a fantastic resource to know more about the history of baseball or watch some of the best moments. One of the videos that could be interesting if you are looking to understand more about the baseball's past is the video "Why do all MLB ballparks differ in size? | Quick Question (MLB Originals)'. In this clip they discuss the development of stadiums for baseball and provide a look of what stadiums were like in the past as well as how the stadium of today is constructed today.

Cable TV and Satellite:

There has never been a better price or simpler to purchase the channels you desire and also pay a reasonable price. Now you can buy bundles of the channels you'd like to see. The satellite TV channel, regardless of whether Dish Network or DirectTV has one of the largest sports packages available that are perfect for the sports enthusiast. One of the best things about satellite TV is it is possible to find any sporting event that is live you want to record and then watch the game no matter which location you're located. Television channels such as ESPN or MLBTV give viewers access to off-market games two or three times a week. If you're looking for something to watch, you can watch it with or through a cable either a satellite or satellite bundle, or different streaming provider.

Facebook:

Facebook is slowly dying. Thanks to apps such as Instagram and Snapchat it's simple to compress a highlight into a smaller size and then publish it on the web. Instagram and Snapchat are able to fill the gaps in the area where Facebook does not. Although Facebook offers the option of posting videos, and occasionally Facebook might show live event, Instagram and Snapchat are more adept at recording highlights of any sport.

Twitter:

Twitter is not usually the most ideal place to view the sports action. However, if you're looking to know the score of your favourite team or watch highlights, Twitter is an excellent platform. If you'd like to follow the team you love it is possible to do that as well. This includes minor league teams too.

TikTok and SpapChat:

TikTok has emerged as the next big social media site. Anyone can create an account and upload any video. This is a precursor to Vine. TikTok is home to a number of baseball video. One of the reasons this app is an effective method for growing the game of baseball is the ability to create a meme within the video. It also gives people who aren't baseball enthusiasts a bit of insight into what happens within the game. Baseball is available on SnapChat is like the one of TikTok as well as Instagram. Uploading your videos on the platform is as simple. The user can create memes from the video and upload it to social media.

Chapter 4: Video Games Featuring Baseball

You can now walk into any video game retailer to purchase a premium baseball game. With stunning graphics and a great games, it's expected to cost around $60.00 to get a tangible version of the baseball video game. The players also do not have to visit the stores since they are able to download the games to their computer.

The Nintendo 64 is not typically thought of as a console to play sports games, but it did feature one of the best-known baseball-related video games. The game featured Major League Baseball featuring Ken Griffey Jr. The game was launched in 1998. game gave gamers a 3-D simulation of baseball but included many of the elements that are the video games in baseball today. This included how you wanted your batter to strike and throwing your pitches in the direction you want within the strike zone.

As a kid, I loved playing the video games of baseball. The first game on video that I ever played was "Home Run King' from Sega. The game taught me about baseball's strategy. I wasn't able to simply beat my computer using speedy pitches or hitting the ball with a hammer. In a sport that carries the tagline "Home Run King," it took more than just hitting home runs. Like in real-life playing baseball, players needed to plan each game. Although this might not have been the greatest video game of baseball however, it did introduce me to the things I had to be able to accomplish, not just with the computer but the things I had to be doing when I was on the field.

MVP Baseball 2005 was my most loved game as an infant. The first time I saw a video game where the coach had the option of yelling at the umpire only to be exiled. Every time I invited guests over, we would be kicked out of our managers and then laugh. The game's designers created a wonderful game by giving the impression that manager was swearing, however there was no sound that could be associated with the sound. One of the best things about the game was that it could play the game that was set in the first half in the early 20th century. As an example, you can have a ball in the Polo Grounds and have the images with both black and white.

In the beginning of games that were video-based Baseball was among the games that sold several cartridges. The very first video game of baseball that could be played in a home was played by Atari's "Home Run' game, which was exclusive to Atari 2600. There were just two fielders and a batter. The graphics were primitive that it appeared as if they could have been created on a T-83 calculator. Then, Atari games got better graphics, and the games started to look closer to what you'd expect to see in a live baseball game.

The time you had the NES as well as the Nintendo Entertainment System came along it was a world away from the graphic design from the norm. It was at least in the last decade of the 1980s. RBI Baseball is the prime instance of this time. It was played as the real game of baseball. The rules were set, as well as an easy A and B button system It was easy to understand and enjoyable to play. Then, a few years later it was the time that Sega Genesis launched. One of the initial games that came out on the system was "Tommy Lasorda Baseball'. It was a 16 bit baseball game with video that changed the sport. It was not just a better game that had superior graphics and sound, but it also featured a famous player backing it and made fans of video games and baseball to purchase an Sega Genesis with a copy of the game.

In 1992, the video game maker SNK launched Baseball Stars 2 for the arcade. It was a significant advancement from Baseball Stars on the NES because it was the very first video games with a 24-bit resolution. It was considered to be one of the top 2D baseball games released during the 90s.

3D gaming was to come during the late 1990s. It was the Nintendo 64, the original PlayStation as well as Sega Saturn Sega Saturn would all show the world how they could accomplish by using 3D graphics. This meant that greater details were put into the players, the baseballs the stadiums and spectators. There was also more control of the pitches you could throw. Fans were delighted with the latest line of games. From Major League Baseball featuring Ken Griffey Jr.' to EA Baseball games the video game of baseball were becoming more popular from the middle of 1990s and into the early 2000s.

The most current baseball games that are available as of 2020 include RBI Baseball 20 and MLB the Show 20. With the advent of 4K graphics and we have implemented all of the rules and tendencies which could occur and can occur in the game, you are able to play realistic baseball games to play on your console. One of the greatest advantages of the latest video games for baseball is the ability to play online with anyone who has an internet connection, version of the game and a game console the game on. Nowadays, you can talk with players as well as live stream your video and upload it online later.

Baseball Movies

For as long as films exist, there have also been movies about sports. Baseball was the ideal game to feature in films. In the beginning of silent films it was a perfect game for comedy. The first silent film on baseball was a documentary titled 'The Ball Game'. The film consisted of video footage of a game played that took place between Reading Coal Heavers and the Newark Bears. The film was made 20 feet from the base bag with the first. In spite of its age, this short film is for no cost and download it on the web.

There were a variety of films during the first half into the second half of 20th Century including 'The Kid From Leftfield" and 1951's version of the film

'Angels from the outfield'. In 1962 the year 1962, a movie was released entitled 'Safe At Home Safe at Home!. In the film, athletes Mickey Mantle and Roger Maris from the New York Yankees star as themselves. It was among the first films that had professional athletes appear in a film. This film was about the story of a Florida kid who swindles the Little League teammates, telling they know Mantle as well as Maris and that he will take the two to the team's banquet. Through this he is taught an crucial lesson on the importance of honesty.

Films from the 1970s and 1980s:

The the first film about a sports team that launched the sport team genre was "The Bad News Bears'. Though it was meant to be a children's movie however, it contained plenty of swear words even for the year 1976. The thing that made this film stand out was the fact that it focused on the entire team instead of focusing on just one particular player. It was focused on the whole team as well as their challenges and their progress. The sequels included two versions of the first film, and both did fairly well.

The film 'The Natural' from 1984 The Natural' was based on the novel by Bernard Malamud in 1952 that was titled the same. Roy Hobbs was an unknown player prior to becoming a member of in the New York Knights. He appears to be astonished by his appearance and develops into a great player with the bat he loves that he named 'Wonderboy'. Hobbs's skills contributed to in helping the New York Knights become a successful team.

The film made $48 million in the theaters and received nominations for four academy awards. These awards were given to the best supporting actress, cinematography and music direction and art direction.

In 1988, the film "Bull Durham" was released in theatres. The film was based on the actual AAA minor league club The Durham Bulls. Even though no of the characters were ever present in the real world, it provided a glimpse into the daily life of players in minor leagues as well as what life is like for players playing in major leagues as well as those that had the possibility of getting to the big leagues.

In 1989, the film "Major League was released and changed the genre of sports movies. It was the very first sports film that incorporated the perfect mix of a comedy about sports and an unpopular story. The film focuses on Cleveland

Indians are Cleveland Indians are the worst team of baseball in the majors and thus are selected to be the bottom of the pack. Like The Bad News Bears', the focus of the film isn't upon one player in particular, rather the entire group as a whole, and finding ways to conquer the challenges they face in and out of the field.

The 90s and movies of the present day:

The 1990s were the time when films about sports like "The Mighty Ducks" made their debut which elevated the sports film category more than it was. The result was a surge of numerous sports films specifically for children. The most famous film released at this time was "The Sandlot'. While it's an baseball-themed film but it was also a mix of many additional elements from a film. The classic film of the 1990s featured a brand new boy known as Scott Smalls. He happens to see children playing the game of baseball in the Sandlot. Scott discovers a space on the left side of the field. When the ball goes in his direction, he doesn't manage to strike the ball, and is snubbed by the kids around him. Following this, Benny finds Scott and invites him back on the field. The second time, Scott gets to know the game and bonds with the players.

As summer progresses, the kids begin getting into problems. In the end, Scott hits his step dad's ball signed by Babe Ruth over the fence. In this moment, Scott is aware of the huge error he made. Nine players are now required to retrieve the ball. The film is more than just a film about baseball. It was an iconic summertime film and what differentiated the film from other sports films was the fact that it included the sport of baseball into something kids played during summertime.

There were two other baseball-themed films made during the 90s. These included Little Big League as well as Angels in the Outfield, not to be mistaken for the 1951 film.

Moneyball is an action film that was based on the way in which players from the Oakland A's won 20 games consecutively and transformed how teams could beat opponents. The film's opening scene is a look at the Athletics Scouting staff looking for ways to determine the best way to take on to replace their main superstars, Johnny Damon, Jason Giambi as well as Jason Isringhausen. Billy Bean, the general manager, finally meets Peter Brand in the Cleveland Indians office and gains an entirely new view of how they can put together an effective baseball team with the budget of a modest one. Peter informs the scouts and managers that they focus on purchasing players, when they should think in terms of buying winnings. Following the break for all-stars, the team is on an unbeaten streak, winning 20 straight games. The film highlights that teams don't require a star player to succeed and it is possible to be successful even in a group of people who may not seem to be the best.

The film "42" made in 2013 was an action-packed documentary on Jackie Robinson's career as a professional baseball player. The film examines the various obstacles and discrimination he needed overcome in order to be a top MLB player, starting his year in 1947. Fans of baseball, old and young will be entertained by this film.

Chapter 5: Locations And Small Markets

New York, Los Angeles Los Angeles, and Chicago are among the top sports markets of all professional sports of the United States. With a variety of teams competing that play the same sport and three cities with at least one sport team that is part of the MLB, NBA, NFL and NHL the fans are offered an array of teams to support. However, this isn't the case in smaller markets like Kansas City and Cincinnati. Both cities do not have teams that compete in any of the main sporting leagues. If players are selected into these kinds of smaller markets however, they usually don't remain lengthy periods of time. The 2015 Kansas City Royals defeated the New York Mets in five games to take home the World Series. What was so impressive about this win was the fact that a tiny market team beat a large market team in winning the World Series. With the help of stars like Alex Gordon, the Royals could easily win despite the fact that they are a smaller market team. The stars of a team with a smaller market depart for cities like Los Angeles, the small-market team is likely to suffer since they're not as appealing to look at in the eyes of their supporters. In the 2016 season it was the case that the Kansas City Royals became one among the teams that were mediocre within Major league baseball, with the record of 81 and 81. The team didn't make it into the playoffs during the following season. Small-market teams face difficulties managing salary caps as well as individual contracts. This is among the reasons they are prone to drop in terms of performance.

The Baltimore Orioles are a prime example of a tiny market team. In

The 2018 season Manny Machado was traded to the LA Dodgers because he would be a free agent by the conclusion of the season. Orioles were aware that they would not afford signing him. When they traded Machado to Dodgers they were in a position to acquire minor league players who could be stars in the future. Later, he would sign to the San Diego Padres as a free agent. In the wake of other star players leaving during the season The Orioles were ranked second worst in the major leagues. The loss of stars like Machado caused a lot of damage to the Orioles in the short-term. To build teams, like the Orioles the team must create new players and then deal with other players. This is often time-consuming as well as costly. Additionally, smaller market teams aren't able to afford the same resources as big market teams like those of the Dodgers and

Yankees. These teams put small markets on the wrong side of trying to recruit free agents.

The Oakland A's are another small-market team. Since they are one of five MLB teams based in California the team is more difficult to bring in fans. In particular, when they operate in an old ballpark. In competition with Bay Area rivals the San Francisco Giants and the San Francisco Giants, teams like the Athletics aren't able to attract players who are free to join the team. They have a lower budget than the majority of teams, they are unable to pay players like Mike Trout $430 million dollars over the course of 12 years. Their strategy to stand out from big market teams is to discover an untapped value for any player they might add to their roster. This could include signing minor leaguers or trading free players.

Small market teams can face difficulties competing with their main market competitors. But, they are able to be successful and even win championships. Additionally, by putting together an organization in a small city, like Kansas City, you give residents in the area an opportunity to witness the big leagues perform.

Racial Integration

Jackie Robinson is regarded as the greatest person to contribute to the fight to end discrimination in all professional sporting. Robinson broke through the racial divide at the start of 1947, being the first African-American to participate for the MLB. Robinson was a player with his team, the Brooklyn Dodgers.

Branch Rickey saw the potential Robinson had. Branch Rickey saw the potential Robinson was able to realize.

Rickey also saw the potential for the future.

Rickey was aware that in order to improve the game of baseball the barrier of race was to be broken. The reason he was attracted by Robinson was his personality. Jackie Robinson wasn't one to become frustrated easily. Even though he was a target of hatred, Robinson was able to get involved and create an impact and break through the barrier between races.

Integration of race not just boosted the game of baseball, but, after the MLB fully became integrated, it only reached new heights.

On the 9th of July, 1948, On the 9th July in 1948, Leroy Robert "Satchel" Paige made his first MLB appearance. Paige was also the most senior pitcher ever to begin a game in major leagues in addition to being the oldest player to make his make his debut in major leagues. Paige spent the majority all of the time in his MLB career as a member of his team, the Cleveland Indians. In addition, he played some years as a member of the St. Louis Browns and his final year with his team, the Kansas City Royals. Satchel Paige was also the longest-running player ever to take part in a match with a 59-year old age.

It was believed that the Negro League was still playing games right up to the mid-1960s. After the MLB was integrated fully it was a time when interest waned so it was decided that the Negro League folded.

Willie Mays is perhaps one of the greatest players of the current era. With 660 homers, the man certainly has earned to be regarded as one of the top players ever. Willie Mays is also remembered for one of the biggest catch ever made in the 1954 World Series. As he played with the New York Giants, a ball hit the center of the field deep. Many thought the ball was going to drop however Willie Mays made the most impressive catch ever made in MLB time. In the blink of an eye, he snatched up the ball, and immediately put it back in the field.

In 1974, Hank Aaron broke Babe Ruth's 714-home run record. Many threats were thrown at his life during the time he was closing to breaking the record. In April of 1974 the 715th homer. He would later hit another 40 home runs over the course of his career and hit 755 total. He held this record for a period of more than 30 years before Barry Bonds broke it in 2007.

From Little League to the Major Leagues

T-Ball also known as Little League is usually the beginning of the process where children begin to learn about organized baseball. It is the place where children progress or discover they don't want to play the sport of baseball. Participation among youth is declining over the last few years. Since sports like basketball, football and hockey gaining popularity, baseball isn't as appealing an activity for youth.

While I was a kid I participated in an organised Little League. The issue in this league was that there was no way to mix the teams. I was a part of the younger children because I just had moved to an area in which I was a player. If you're starting an structured Little League program, you need to mix teams to help the younger players get acquainted alongside the experienced players.

High School Baseball:

High school students being on the baseball team of their varsity is an exciting experience. Although it isn't the most well-known sports in high school, it's nonetheless attractive to players, parents, students as well as people living within the area. This is an improvement to Little League because now you play seven-inning games with more competitive opponents.

There is a major distinction the fact that, at this stage in their careers, players are making baseball their primary game, which makes more competitive. Teams that have great players could be able to have Major League scouts at their matches.

College Baseball:

There are a variety of NCAA colleges with baseball teams. Ranging from division I team all the way to Division III teams, nearly every university and college is home to a baseball team. For many athletes in college, it could be their first time they've performed in front of live television. It can be thrilling as well as nerve-wracking for students. For many players it's the first time that they have played the nine-inning format. There are no metal bats and bats, however this time, they are playing using the exact regulations as the MLB.

Single A Minor League Baseball:

Single-A Minor League baseball is the first time ballplayers have been paid. Although it's not much however, it's an excellent beginning for young players who could go on into eventually the Big

Leagues. As their earnings are small, single-A players will usually have to share a home in a home with a family they are able living expenses or share a room with several teammates. One of the main differences between college and major leagues is the fact that many minor league matches aren't broadcast. A small-town club usually includes a minor league squad and it's a cheap option alternative to traveling for long distances for a Major League stadium to see an event.

Double AA Minor League Baseball:

Double AAA Minor League baseball doesn't differ significantly than Single A. There is only one difference that the majority of Double AA pitchers that play with an affiliate of a National League affiliate, now must hit, and cannot be allowed to have the DH take the bat for their. In the case of, say, you're playing Double AA baseball for the Springfield Cardinals, the pitcher must now bat whenever they play. There are many players who move from minors to majors from this point. If players want to go up into Triple AAA or sent back to Single A you will find various skill levels within Double AA.

Triple AAA Minor League Baseball:

Triple AAA players are a step away from playing in the major leagues. For

Triple AAA players, the median wage is $80,000 annually. For some the salary is a life altering experience and you'll be able to be content with that amount of money. Players are playing in more populated cities and bigger stadiums. What can make Triple AAA interesting, is that the players could get called up to play an entire game, or even substitute for an injured player, and later be sent back down. However, some players could be called up to be able to become superstars.

The Major Leagues:

The 28 cities of North America hold the 30 Major League baseball teams. New York as well as Chicago each have two teams. If a player from either team makes it to the top of the leagues, this is a goal that will never to be realized even only for a few games. The minimum wage for the league will be $565,500 during the season 2020. The pressure is higher on players to be successful since all games will be broadcast for national and local broadcasters and stadiums could be filled to capacity of more than 50,000 spectators.

The majority of baseball players will never get closer to the big leagues however, many players try. Major League teams connect small towns with big cities, and connect all their teams in the area. Nothing beats going to the stadium of your preferred Major League team. The standard of their play can be top-notch, even when your team has a poor performance. Each player who has come out of the college or minors has shown their worth as a great player who can compete with others who are professional athletes.

Chapter 6: International Leagues

There are numerous other professional leagues that are not part of the MLB. There is, for instance, the Colombian Professional Baseball League and the Mexican Pacific League. The other professional leagues that range across Asian nations to South American Countries have mostly similar rules with there are some minor differences. For example, in Japan, for instance in the Japanese Baseball League, players must adhere to certain restrictions and may be required adhere to specific rules of dress.

There are some commonalities between international leagues and MLB. They all use a designated hitter policy. The Mexican Pacific League, the rules are the same as Major League baseball. The designated hitter is within the league. There are it is not a pitcher's game, and many other rules are similar to Major League baseball.

The KBO (Korean Baseball Organization) the designation of a batter is an all-encompassing principle across every team. Similar to the MLB the KBO uses wooden bats, and they have nine innings per game without counting additional innings.

Season Structure

A hundred times 100 is an impressive amount. Baseball players playing over 100 games in a season is not easy. The MLB is the most long-running season of North American Professional sports with 162 games. This doesn't even include playoffs or the World Series. This is the 81 home games as well as an additional 81 away games. Also, there is a chance that teams will have to play in a 163rd match in order to qualify for a wildcard slot. At first in the past, the MLB group was able to play only 154 games.

The maximum number of games that can be played during a normal MLB year is around 120. If you have just 120 games in the regular season to be played, that allows baseball to have a bit more time to focus on the summer months and also allows them to not play as often against the NFL during the regular season. Also, I suggest you maintain the playoff series in the same length as it currently is.

The length of the season:

The NBA as well as the NHL both have roughly the same total number of games with the teams playing 82 games. One of the biggest problems with the MLB is the fact that they don't realize that even the most dedicated supporters aren't likely to be watching every game. Reducing the season's schedule to 120 games for each team sounds reasonable, especially when there are rainy days and delays due to rain. If you have a game that is raining out, you could shift your schedule around further and make use of one of your days off to play the game instead of having two games. Additionally, with more available time allocated to teams it is likely to be more feasible. Teams can perform better with the benefit of more time off. The best thing about playing a season of 120 games is that baseball will have lesser competition to watch throughout the season.

The teams do not match up against one another. There were 30 MLB teams in 2020.

In the year 2019 it was a year of two tightly-knit divisions: The AL East and the NL Central. This is unfair because it means the fact that both teams aren't playing against each other during the year. Interleague games are strictly limited to just a few games each season. If you increase interleague play, it would even out your playing surface.

It is possible that the Washington Nationals may have to take on a team that is strong, such as that of the Boston Red Sox, while the St. Louis Cardinals get to play a less powerful team, such as that of the Detroit Tigers. The latter could provide the Cardinals an advantage in the event that both Nationals as well as the Cardinals were involved in an open wildcard race. If you'd like to have an even and fair season the MLB must have every team match up for a minimum of one series every season.

The duration of games is also a factor in an extended season. The majority of games today run around three hours.

There are many ideas regarding how to speed the pace of play. The only thing that may fail is implementing the concept of a pitching clock. A pitching clock is the pitcher's responsibility to make the pitch within a specific period of date that the pitcher is able to receive the ball. It's not a good concept because it is playing a different ball game. The game wasn't intended to be played with the concept of a clock. What is required is players not to put the ball in play in the event that there's nobody on base. They'll get out. They should bring the ball back from the pitcher as soon as they can to allow them to continue playing and not waste the time.

Complex Rules

There are a myriad of complicated rules that govern baseball. The designated hitter as well as the double switch may appear confusing for a beginner to baseball. Many people don't realize the fact that in the National League, the pitcher is the one who hits himself, with no exceptions in the case of the double switch, or if a manager calls an in-pitch player. Double switch occurs when the pitcher gets replaced by an alternate pitcher. However, an additional player is substituted for one of the fielders simultaneously. The manager can alter the batting order in such a way that the replacement player is at the position of the pitcher within the batting order, while the pitcher plays at the position of the fielder. The manager can utilize the pitcher for a couple of innings before his place on the order is filled. In that case, the manager may employ a pinch-hitter to the pitcher. He will then choose a relief pitcher for the following innings.

Most often, this occurs in the last innings of a game.

A good example is if the Nationals play with the Mets while the Nationals have lost by one run. In the seventh pitch of the 7th. Max Scherzer is on the mound, and is becoming exhausted. The manager notices that and decides to replace him with Sean Dolittle. But, Sean Dolittle will be the first to bat during the next inning, even if there is a alteration in pitching. In order to prevent him from becoming an easy option for the start of the seventh inning, he'd also have to be replaced by another player in the field for example, the shortstop. This allows the coach to alter the order of batting. The manager can place the new shortstop at the ninth spot of the order of batting and then replace Sean Dolittle where the shortstop hit.

If you're in the American League, you don't require the double switch since the DH plays for the pitcher and can be placed anyplace within the batting order. American League managers don't have to worry about double switches, unless they're playing at the National League park.

The one thing that separates the DH rule from other types of interleague play within other professional sports is that one conference/division/league uses it while the other does not.

My opinion on the DH rules:

The American League and the National League are expected to be similar. If you are in the MLB offers an all-inclusive DH or has no DH altogether It should be identical for teams in the American League and the National League. In this way, neither team will be disadvantaged when playing or against or an American League team or a National League team. There is an argument to have the pitchers strike, having the DH rule in both leagues will take burden off pitchers. As they will not being hitting, they'll become less likely to suffer injuries. Pitchers are also able to focus on the reason they made it to the MLB initially in the first place, and that's their pitching. In the beginning, from Little League to the Majors the majority of pitchers never even step in to bat. If you permit pitchers to concentrate in pitching, you'll be able to see better games, both from the offensive as well as defense. You can also place more veteran players in the DH position to ensure they are active without having them take the field.

The rule of the infield fly:

Infield fly rules are an acceptable fly ball, or pop-up, which could be tackled by any of the players in the infield easily. This includes the pitcher and the catcher. This is a decision that is left to the umpire when there's a single out more and there are at least two people at the base. The umpire may call the batter out when it seems that an infielder is likely to be able to catch the ball. Infield fly rules keep playing even since the team in defense cannot allow the ball to drop and play a double game. The runner can move forward without risk, or remain on their own.

Switch-hitting:

The process of switching hits can become complicated since it is possible for a batter to hit either side but change sides of the plate during the middle of a count provided that the batter announces time and informs the umpire his plans are. In addition, a hitter may come up and strike on either side during duration of an entire game, then during the following at-bat, the batter may switch to the opposite side.

This is a good rule of thumb when you consider it in comparison to many other games. Basketball players may be right handed, however, you do not have shoot using your left hand. Shooting can be done with the hand you hold with your left. This happened once during basketball games, the moment Tracey Mcgrady hit an open shot with the left side of his hand. It's not easy to switch-hit and difficult, but it allows anyone to choose about where and when to strike when at the box for batters.

The Balk:

Balks are illegal move by a pitcher which causes an advantage on players who are runner(s). If an opponent throws the ball in the air before it gets at the batter's feet, this can result in a balk. Each player advances one base. If it's an accident, it's considered a balk. Another method to make a mistake is if the pitcher performs a movement in connection with the pitch however, they fail to complete the pitch. This could be the most frequent method of getting the balk ruled. A umpire could also decide to call balks when the pitcher does not pause before making the call.

It can be difficult to explain balk to those who aren't an avid fan of baseball could become a bit difficult. It's not just that simple. is a source of frustration for many people who are new to baseball. Some may even wonder why a runner should be allowed to go 90 feet faster because of a pitcher's error. The reason for this law was enacted to the beginning of 19th century was to make sure runners did not get fooled by pitchers in attempts to take runners off bases effortlessly.

It is my opinion that this rule must evolve, or perhaps alter. In the event that the balk rules was to be changed, this will give the player more choice regarding how he/she will deliver the ball. Furthermore, umpires will be less likely to miss an error if one or more aspects that define balks were changed.

Chapter 7: Confusion Baseball With Softball

Most people believe the sole difference between softball and baseball are pitching with a hand and the fact that softballs weigh more than baseballs. It's far than the reality. While these two points could represent the primary difference, there are different distinctions. In particular, there's no pitcher's mound when playing softball. The rubber of the pitcher is an unmarked circle. It is the pitcher's responsibility to throw pitches through this region. Softball players can't be a lead runner before taking the ball away. It gives defenses an advantage in getting the runner off. Even though the runner might not be able to run as long sprint if they were running in a baseball diamond however, defenses can better stop runners from advancing into scoring positions. A different aspect is the distance between the home plate and the fence. The distance required to hit a homerun typically is less than 300 feet. on a softball field and the distance between home plate to fence in major leagues may vary between 315 feet. up to more than 400 feet.

Dead balls and live balls:

On the 14th of October, 2015 on October 14th, 2015 the Texas Rangers faced the Toronto Blue Jays in Rogers Center. It was among the most exciting baseball games that you can imagine. In spite of many erroneous plays as well as home runs, it proved to be among the most thrilling matches in MLB the history of baseball.

The initial six innings seemed as if it was a typical playoff until the seventh inning came around, it was when the game got more fascinating. Two batters are dismissed at the first. Then Shin-Soo Choo stepped up to the plate. At 2-2, the score was set, Russel Martin accidentally threw the ball over his bat, and it went live. The runner was able to score on the third.

The incident was so confusing that the umpires even had to verify the meaning of the rules. What was the reason for it to be a live ball in accordance with the rule is that the ball was never returned to the pitcher, and Choo didn't intend to interfer with the throwing. The only person who knew about it was Harold Reynolds, who was the announcer to announce the game, interpreted the correct answer. All the other players including the umpires believed that the ball was at first it was a dead ball.

When a batter deliberately interferes with the ball, then batter will be out of the game and the ball becomes dead. A typical dead ball that is in the condition where the batter isn't able to play with the ball, would include a batter fouling or hitting a ball. The ball striking the batter. Whatever the place where the ball ends up following that point, the ball is dead.

Basketball has a few of the most complicated rules that any game can have. One thing that makes a game like basketball a lot easier to grasp is the fact that you only need to keep moving until you are able to play the ball, or even shoot it. Even though basketball might have complicated rules, like the violation of three seconds however, it's nowhere far from being as complicated as baseball.

Bunting Foul:

When a player is at base, teams typically attempt to bunt in order to move the player into scoring position. Bunting gives teams that are trailing an advantage in a do-or-die circumstance. The only thing you should not do is repeatedly bunting in foul. If a batter is hit by two strikes during the count and then fouls on the third strike, the batter is struck out. One exception is when the batter pulls back the bat and the ball strikes the bat, it's not an foul ball strike number three. It's just an additional foul ball. It can be confusing when you think about the fact that batters are able to continuously take balls off the field, as long as their swing is full. Why was this rule adopted? The reason for this rule is in order to stop the fielding team from losing out. If a batter stays in the batter's box for a long time with little effort, it doesn't just give the team batting them an advantage unfairly, but also slows down the speed of play.

Stadiums

Prior to the stadiums that we see today the games of baseball were played on the field. The stadiums of the 1800s were similar to the base path with its outlines and a lawn that was flat. There weren't many benches or bleachers to sit within. The majority of the time, there wasn't an outfield fence. Field players had to chase after the ball, no matter which direction the ball went. In the absence of a fence, balls would fly and strike random objects in the distance from where they were. As baseball teams made their way into the city and stadiums were designed, they required fences in order to stop this. Fences, in turn, helped to create the idea of the homerun. Fences were constructed to increase the number of seats sold in the stadium as well as to generate profits.

Major League baseball stadiums were one of the most famous stadiums in the period of American sports. Ebbett's Field and Polo Grounds are probably the two iconic venues for sports during that era. The two venues hosted numerous world championships and some NFL championships. At the beginning of large sports venues and stadiums, both NFL as well as MLB teams shared the same stadium, if they were each located within the same town. The practice continued to the start of the 2019 season for both leagues. The Oakland Coliseum was one of the few venue to host both an NFL as well as an MLB team in the same stadium.

If it's about economics, it is economically advantageous to continue this model of business and let every MLB as well as NFL teams playing in the same town have the same venue. It keeps the costs of construction of stadiums down since cities are required to pay for hosting two teams at the same stadium.

The reason the new stadiums do not have their NFL as well as MLB teams in the same venue is due to of their structure. The football field is rectangular while an MLB field is diamond. In the past, when cities like Oakland and Philadelphia had these kinds of stadiums, maintenance teams were required to change the football field into an baseball field, or the reverse. This was cost-effective because each football owner as well as owners of baseball would share the cost and share the cost.

The stadium of the first generation:

The first half into the second half of century 20 saw an opportunity to modern sports stadiums. The initial Yankee Stadium was built in 1923. It could accommodate as many as 70,000 fans. The initial Yankee Stadium was the biggest arena until the 1932 season. In 1932, Cleveland Municipal Park, home to the Cleveland Indians was built to hold 78,000 fans.

One of the most famous stadiums that emerged from the very first generation were Wrigley Field and Fenway Park. They have more than 100 years worth of tradition, numerous pennants, as well as World Series victories, these two stadiums are an examples of what a venue should look like.

Fenway Park was built in 1912 in Boston. It is Fenway the longest-running ballpark operating in the present. Fenway Park is one of the most compact modern stadiums with regard to seats and field size.

Wrigley Field was built in 1914, originally known as Weeghman Park and has hosted the Chicago Cubs from 1916 to today. In the beginning the stadium was renamed Cubs Park. After the team was acquired from William Wrigley Jr. in 1921, the stadium was the name changed one final time. It was changed to Wrigley field. It can accommodate 41,649 spectators. When the stadium was in its early times, it was not common to find a stadium for sports that could have that capacity.

The Second Generation of Stadiums:

From the 1960s until the 1980s saw the beginning of the second generation of stadiums for sports.

In 1962, the New York Mets played their debut two seasons at Polo Grounds. In 1964, Shea Stadium finished construction and the Mets were there for the following 45 seasons from 1964 through 2008. With the Mets being there for the full 45 years The New York Jets played there for a total of 20 seasons between 1964 and 1983. New stadiums like Shea as well as Veterans Memorial Stadium in Philadelphia were designed to handle both baseball and football matches. This latest generation of stadiums is a clever way to have baseball and football clubs from the exact same town use the same venue.

In 1966 year 1966, the Houston Astrodome was built. It also was the first sports arena for professionals that used artificial turf, more commonly referred to as Astroturf. It was also home to the

Houston Oilers would also play in the stadium from 1968 to 1996.

Modern Day Stadiums:

The modern-day stadium era was born in the month of April on when players from the Baltimore Orioles played the Cleveland Indians at Oriole Park. Oriole Park was the first of the new generation that had straight-edged walls. The arena was initially designed as a place for two teams: Baltimore Colts and Baltimore Colts and the Baltimore Orioles. After the city was able to secure enough money to finance the project however, the Colts went to Indianapolis. The new stadium to be built specifically in the interest of the Orioles. The initial design was an "ashtray" (circular stadium) that was similar to the stadiums of Veterans Stadium in Philadelphia.

In 2001, PNC park was constructed for The Pittsburgh Pirates. The stadium was an change from their earlier design stadium Three Rivers Stadium. Along with a stunning views from the Allegheny River from the upper deck located on the third base side PNC Park provided a variety of facilities, such as more view over the playing field.

Citi Field located in Queens, NY was a amazing feat of architecture after it was built in the year 2009. It was built using elements from the former Shea Stadium, Ebbets Field as well as The Polo Grounds. In particular, all seats are in green, the facade on the outside is similar to that of Ebbets Field and an apple for home runs can be found on the exterior, near the main entrance to the stadium. There is another in center field. The overall cost for building Citi Field was around $1.07 billion.

The latest arena can be found at Globe Life Field, located in Arlington Texas, home of the Texas Rangers. The stadium was built for around $1.1 billion to construct.

Each baseball field is unique in its dimensions. Every outfield is unique. The distance required to hit a homerun varies across stadiums and every stadium comes with its own distinct attributes. As an example, there's trains that run each time an Astros player hit home runs in Minute Maid Park. One thing all professional baseball stadiums lack today is a curving outfield fence.

Chapter 8: International Stadiums

International stadiums could appear quite similar to MLB stadiums, or very different from the MLB stadiums. In Japan Koshien Stadium is one of them. Koshien Stadium. It is a unique stadium that has an all-dirt infield. There is no grass on the infield, it could surely provide for an interesting games. Additionally, there are a number of domed stadiums within Japan's Japanese Baseball League. One thing that differentiates the stadiums of MLB Stadiums is their curved outfield wall. The majority of the 30 MLB stadiums currently are constructed with straight edges and have eliminated the fences that are curved. However, in Japan, in the Japanese leagues, you'll continue to see curved outfield walls inside the stadiums.

Within the Mexican Pacific League, there aren't indoor domed stadiums. There are only outdoor ones. Within Korea, which is part of the Korea Baseball Organization, there several stadiums. There are indoor dome stadiums, and outdoor stadiums.

Taxpayers:

The tax payers who reside in cities that are home to professional baseball teams often get "fleeced" for the latest design of stadiums, or maintenance for the existing ones. Imagine that your favorite artist is performing on tour and they don't travel to your town until certain conditions are fulfilled. Why is it not that the duty of the taxpayers to support the band you love? But what if the taxpayer doesn't like the group? What is the reason why a taxpayer should need to pay more taxes to enjoy your favourite band's performance live? This can also be said about cities with a significant sports teams. Consider a city for example like Miami and they are home to teams across all the four major leagues of sports. The 2012 season saw the Florida Marlins became the Miami Marlins and relocated into a new stadium. To allow this plan to be completed, taxpayers would have to foot the costs to the city as well as the state in order to finance the stadium.

Presently, the Miami Marlins have one of the most disappointing attendance records in the past five seasons and always rank at the bottom of the list this means that the taxpayers don't have any interest in visiting the stadium they have bought for them.

Before this, was the fact that the Dolphins and Marlins each played at Sun

Life Stadium. In the latter part of the 1990s and the early 2000s, the teams shared the facilities of the stadium.

If new stadiums are constructed and are constructed, regardless of whether it's a double stadium or single-use stadium, the taxpayers of state and cities indirectly contribute to the building for the new stadium. The taxpayers shouldn't have to be subsidized by teams that may not go to. According to forbes.com The MLB made a record $10.7 billion in the year 2019. The four leagues of major sports have a amount of around $40 billion.

Every industry that earns millions of dollars isn't receiving taxpayer money. Imagine taxpayers paying for video game firms like Nintendo. Many people would be upset by the fact that their tax-payer money was directed towards an

American company and one that people might not wish to join. Private businesses shouldn't be subsidised by the people of the state or city.

My personal opinion on what I think should occur:

I believe taxpayers shouldn't play a role in assisting billion-dollar industries. The way to go is that the sports teams, be it the MLB or another major organization in sports and should seek to raise money on sites like GoFundMe or their owners can utilize their own funds to construct new stadiums so that more people can watch their matches. Recently, some owner have made use of their own money for the building of stadiums. I also recommend that when teams of baseball build new stadiums, that they make sure that the cost of construction is to a minimum, and maintain a high level of excellence.

Statistics in Baseball

Baseball and statistics are just like butter and bread. While I was a kid I was learning about division and percentages by watching batsmen's batting averages and their number of at-bats during each season, as well as the number of hits they took. I then used the total number of hits and then divided by the total at-bats of the entire season, to determine the average batting of every player. In my college years, the final assignment for my economics course in computational computing included creating a baseball-specific sabermetrics software that was written in Python.

In the beginning, for kids who are learning fundamental arithmetic and decimals and division Baseball is a fantastic sport to demonstrate real-world instances of this. Parents and their children a opportunity to connect. If a parent is arguing through math issues with their child, they could create math-related problems of their own using the data from previous games of the season in order to determine an athlete's Earned Run Average (ERA) and batting average.

One method utilized to aid them in learning numbers and statistics is by teaching them the various acronyms, and the methods to calculate each one of them. As an example, you could explain to them that ERA is determined by adding up the total amount of earned runs that the pitcher pitched, divided by the total number of innings pitched by the pitcher divided by 9.

There's never been a more perfect time to study any topic you'd like. With the advent online and websites that are based on research it is possible to locate any information or historical piece regarding Major League and Minor league baseball players. Check out this website: https://www.baseball-almanac.com/

Also, check out the audiobook 'Big Data Baseball' from audiobooks.com if you want to learn more about baseball statistics: https://www.audiobooks.com/audiobook/big-data-baseball-math-miracles-and-the-end-of-a-20-year-losing-streak/233575

Take your children to a ball game. One of the best ways to learn about playing the game is by attending these games. Attending an actual baseball match is a great method to educate your children how to play. It is possible to purchase a game and instruct them on how to record the game with an official scorecard which records every strike, run or out of the game for each the player. However, no matter what the end result is, you need to teach your children that it's just one game, and it's a fantastic game that is enjoyed by all who watch.

What changed the way statistics have shaped baseball?

The majority of people will consider Billy Bean of the Oakland Athletics who used stats to change the way we play of baseball. In reality, baseball sabermetrics were utilized long before the time of this. The difference was the case that Billy Bean had discovered something not visible to the naked eye that teams were not using. The stats they utilized included players' On Base Percentage (OBP) as well as on base plus slugging (OPS).

Additionally they discovered great pitchers, such as Chad Bradford who pitched using the submarine pitching type. Many teams turned him down because of his inexperience and his speed was around the mid-80 range. His subdued approach made him a successful pitcher.

Earl Weaver, the manager of the Baltimore Orioles for their 1970 World Series victory used a "Moneyball-based system" prior to in 2002, the Oakland A's. Earl Weaver had only a handful of stars, however the team did have players that could score on base and take quick hits. Weaver knew that it's better to allow a player to take the chance to walk rather to make an error. The stance was instrumental in helping the Orioles to win more than 100 games during the season.

Following the 2002 season Stats like on base Percentage (OBP) along with OBP (OPS) were employed in evaluating prospects. The "Moneyball" system expanded far beyond the baseball field. This method of gathering data can be used today to evaluate job applicants as well as companies and determine what stocks are likely to succeed. There are many biases that can lead us to certain notions about people. Utilizing a sabermetrics tool like "Moneyball" can help to delve deeper into information and uncover things many people wouldn't take into consideration.

The 2013 Pittsburgh Pirates broke their 20-season losing streak. They had a record of 94 and 68 and 68, the Pirates were also able to make the playoffs. The Pirates took advantage of the concept of "Moneyball" and also incorporated defensive strategies along with offensive strategies used in players of the Oakland A's. The Pirates utilized defensive shifts on the middle of the field to bring players out. They finished first in "out efficacy" in that particular season.

The perfect analogy for baseball to live your life

There's no sport better that can be used as a metaphor to describe real-life situations. Like, for example, a practice in baseball is similar to attending class or work as you're practicing and doing the work required to make improvements in the quality of your life.

It is not uncommon for baseball to go the as life, except that some unexpected incidents occur to our lives. Similar to not getting a ground ball you could miss an easy part of a test, or make a misstep on the job. Similar to the baseball team is required to brush your head and mentally prepare for the next phase of your life. There's a chance that you'll be successful with the next step or not be successful However, you need to be ready for anything.

Similar to making a homerun You can also enjoy a great moment and hit it right off the field. (Pun intended). If you're taking on the task it's impossible to know the outcome you'll receive. Much like when presenting an assignment for class or your job, you'll never be able to be aware of the outcome until the moment it occurs. Therefore, do your best to be prepared for to be surprised.

Chapter 9: What Can You Do To Increase The Popularity Of Baseball?

Baseball isn't the most loved sport yet there's plenty that you can accomplish to improve the game. One of the most effective ways to promote the game of baseball is to wear the jersey you love and a cap. Make sure that people know which teams and who the players are. Attend the games, especially for those who live in smaller market or possess a minor league soccer club located in the town. When you go to matches, you help grow your game by creating demand for additional games.

Participating in the neighborhood Little League team is also an ideal way to show your support for the sport of baseball. If your Little Leaguer is willing assistance with your yard or even sell baked goods, offer some encouragement. In addition to supporting the local Little League team, but you're also encouraging entrepreneurial spirit in the children of those teams.

Watching the Little League World Series:

Although it's not the Olympics or a high-end baseball team however it's an excellent way to help the sport on an international scale. A lot of countries remain involved with the sport, like Japan, Mexico, and majority of countries that are located in South America. In having the Little League World Series televised globally, you open new territories to the game. As an example, if a Brazilian Little League team is taking part at the Little League World Series, however, St. Lucia is not taking part in the Series If they broadcast the games internationally, citizens of St. Lucia can still be able to watch the matches and also get a team to play for the upcoming season. Television broadcasts show other nations what it's like to play and encourages newcomers take part in the sport.

If you're a parent and you want to set up a play area for them within your yard. Ask your friends to come to barbecues, and then enjoy playing with the children. It's a great idea during holidays like the Fourth of July.

Baseball books:

There are plenty of baseball-related books that you can read and discuss with your fellow fans.

The most popular baseball books is "Shoeless Joe," composed by W.P. Kinsella. This novel was the basis for the film 'Field of Dreams'. In the novel, the protagonist is a farmer called Ray Kinsella went about his mornings working at his farm, and also selling his produce. One day, he's guided by a spirit who tells him to construct the baseball fields. Later, in the book in which he is a character, he comes across J.D. Salinger and the two embark to the edge of adventure. In the next chapter, Salinger and the duo encounter a ghost player from baseball known as "Moonlight" Graham.

A different baseball book is "Calico Joe' written by John Grisham. A young man by the title from Joe Castle is seen as one of the best players to ever play during Major League baseball. The fans of all baseball idolize his name, and that includes a young boy called Paul Tracey. However, things take an unexpected turn when his father, Warren Tracey, throws a pitch that alters everything in their lives.

There are many biographies on players, such as Derek Jeter and Cal Ripken Jr. who is a great choice for newcomers when they are looking to understand more about the sport or about a particular player. If you're interested in learning the best ways to improve your skills There are a variety of guides that offer strategies and tips to help you teach or develop the baseball abilities of your.

Create baseball as a mainstay in your locality:

The idea of forming a community softball or baseball club is an excellent option if you are looking to expand the game. Additionally, it connects you to your community, and helps you meet your neighbors. It also helps you develop and build on your teamwork abilities regardless of your age. If you can play with a new group of people, it boosts your certainty that you will be able to collaborate with any person, in and out of the field.

If you do not have an area for baseball or softball make one. While I'm not suggesting you need to construct fields like the one in the film "Field of Dreams", however if you have land, or are able to invest in the land to start your own baseball business and you can afford it, you must take the initiative to build it.

The most economical methods is to purchase some baseball equipment together with a set of bases. When you've got all your equipment, and if there's the space or live located in rural areas arrange the bases. Then bring a few people together to enjoy the game. There's no need to organize a game and you can play at any time you'd like.

My top 15 unforgettable moments from the past 30 years.

1.) Ken Griffey and Ken Griffey Jr. hit back-to-back home runs:

The 14th of September, 1990 Ken Griffey and his son Ken Griffey Jr. both hit home runs from back to back. On the 14th of September, 1990, Ken Griffey and his son hit home runs. Seattle Mariners were playing the California Angels in Anaheim. It was the bottom of the 1st inning. Ken Griffey Sr. got a home run that scored two runs which make the Mariners ahead 2 - 0. Then, Ken Griffey Jr. hit a solo homer that added to the lead. No other sport has ever seen the same thing take place. It was an unusual occasion in baseball that had did not have before, and it hasn't occurred since. The father and son compete together in a game on the same team, they each accomplished the same feat.

2) Ripken's record-breaking moment:

Doing more than 2000 times of something is a huge accomplishment. The feat of playing 2000 times in one go is a different. The 6th of September, 1995 Cal Ripken Jr. played his 2131st Major league match in one row. The previous record set by Lou Gehrig of 2130 straight games played was broken on that evening. The thing that made the record-breaking event special was that, after the bottom of the 5th inning Oriole Park, Ripken shook every person on the 1st row. There hasn't been a single other player to do something similar to this in the history of any game. In addition, to cap the day off, Ripken hit home runs.

Over 3000 hits the World Series title, and an old-fashioned record, Cal Ripken Jr. is likely to be remembered as the most famous Baltimore Oriole ever.

3.) The Cubs won their first World Series of the year. 2016 World Series:

The fact that you can go 108 years without doing something can be considered a major accomplishment either good or bad or just plain indifferent. Most people don't even live for a century. In the case of those who belong to the Chicago Cubs, it was the 108th year of their misery. The moment they beat their American League rivals, the Chicago White Sox won the World Series in 2005, it provided the Cubs the hope they could see that their World Series drought could also be over. However, that didn't happen for an additional eleven years.

The curse of the billy goat is among the most bizarre stories from American sports. There are various versions of the story. The story goes that a man bought two tickets for himself as well as one for his billy goat. But, when he arrived at the stadium, he was refused access even though he purchased tickets to his goat. The man was so angry, the curse was placed on the Cubs to ensure that they could never be able to win a World Series again. Over the course of 108 years it appeared the curse had been real.

In the year 2016, the Los Angeles Dodgers and the Chicago Cubs were two of the most popular teams of the National League. They Chicago Cubs had a record of 103-58. The Dodgers were able to record 90 - 70. The Cubs beat Los Angeles Dodgers Los Angeles Dodgers to win their first championship since 1945.

If it was announced that the Cleveland Indians won the 2016 American League

Pennant, the World Series would become a race to determine who wants to finish the World Series drought the most. It was the Cleveland Indians hadn't won the pennant since 1997, and had not been crowned the World Series since 1948. The moment they Indians were up by three games to one during the World Series It appeared to be a sign that Cubs fans had to wait at the very least for another year before they could taste the glory of the World Series and break the curse.

In the final night of the game 5 at Wrigley Field at Wrigley Field, the Cubs started to turn the game around. Even though the Indians had a quick one-nil lead during the second inning they would lose the game since the Cubs added three runs at the bottom of fourth. The Indians could get another score in the sixth however it was not enough. The

Cubs won game 5 by a the score 3 - 2. With players like Dexter Fowler, Anthony Rizzo and John Lester to help them to win the game The Cubs were now in the prime chance to win in the World Series.

Following their win in game 5 in the 5th game, the Cubs returned to Cleveland for game 6, which they won. The series was being tied at 3 games and the Indians were still home field advantage in game 7. The Cubs beat the Indians 8-7 however, it took them 10 innings to prevail. In the aftermath of winning the World Series, Cubs fans would be able to rejoice once they realized that their World Series drought was over.

4) The Red Sox 2004 World Series Win:

"The curse of Bambino is among the most intriguing stories from American sports. The year 1919 was the time Babe Ruth was traded from 1918's World

Series Champions, the Boston Red Sox, to the New York Yankees. The manager of the Red Sox at the time, Harry Frazee, sold Babe Ruth to the Yankees to get cash for his talent. In the absence of thinking about baseball it appeared as if the action cursed all Red Sox. They Red Sox had not won the World Series since 1918.

In 2004, the 2004 AL pennant was among the most intriguing pennants in the 2000s. Stars such including Johnny Damon, Manny Ramirez and David Ortiz, the Red Sox could have all the equipment at their disposal to be able to win in the World Series.

The Red Sox came into the playoffs of 2004 sporting one of their greatest records in history. The team had 98 wins and only 64 loss. The first team they faced were The Anaheim Angels who got into the wildcard spot. They had a tough battle against their opponents, the Red Sox, losing the series by a score of 3 to 0.

The next opponent they faced was their longest-running rival, they were the New York Yankees. The Yankees included numerous team members as their initial family, with the exception of Alex Rodriguez who had been transferred to The Texas Rangers. The game would run all seven games. When they Boston Red Sox went down by three to zero in the game, they managed to bounce back to win the remaining four games. The team won the series by 4 games to 3. It was the first ever time and the only one in the history of baseball that a team in the playoffs took a win having lost the first three games. Nobody could have predicted Boston to finish winning the game.

When that the Red Sox won the American League Pennant The majority of the doubts over them taking home in the World Series began to dissipate. But, there were concerns in the minds of certain baseball enthusiasts about the fact that this curse present. In the next few months, the naysayers proved incorrect. They were proved wrong when the Red Sox swept the St. Louis Cardinals and went on winning their fourth World Series. This was the debut World Series win in 86 years.

5) The Chicago White Sox 2005 World Series Win:

There is an allegation that the year 1919 was when Arnold Rothstein had Joe Jackson as well as seven other players fail to win in the 1919 World Series on purpose. The evidence of this isn't conclusive. It would be the final occasion for Chicago White Sox would be in the World Series. Chicago White Sox would be playing in the World Series until 1959.

In the past that followed, both Chicago Cubs and the White Sox faced struggles, and were not great. While neither team won their first World Series since 1917, the years that followed proved to be a disaster for those White Sox. The 1950s were their most successful decade in the 20th century when they took home the AL Pennant in 1959. However, after that it was over, the White Sox mostly had either poor or average seasons.

In 2005, the White Sox would steamroll their way to winning the World Series, having only been defeated once by their opponents, the Anaheim Angels. They would go on to win the World Series. White Sox would win their first pennant since the year 1959. Then they'd have to face Lance Berkman and the Houston Astros. The Series is not a problem to Chicago's White Sox. Without the White Sox star designated hitter, Frank Thomas, Chicago did manage to take down the Astros.

6.) Mariano Rivera being inducted into the hall of fame in a unanimous manner:

Mariano Rivera is regarded as the most effective closer in Major League Baseball history. Rivera was a player for 17 years in all, of which were with the New York Yankees. After winning five World Series with the New York Yankees nobody else was called to more frequently in the postseason in the 90s and in the early 2000s to close games. The year 2013 was the last time Rivera was a participant in the final all-star game, and would quit alongside Andy Pettitte that year.

In all the accomplishments Rivera did, he was aware that it would only be an issue of time before Rivera was admitted to the hall of famous. In the year 2019 Rivera was the first and the only MLB player who was voted into the hall fame in a unanimous vote.

7.) Barry Bonds' home record for runs:

Barry Bonds started his career playing for his team the Pittsburgh Pirates and played for the team for seven seasons. The record holder is currently held by Barry Bonds for having the highest number of career home runs. A career-high 762 homers, only the top hitters even come close to matching the record. In the beginning of his seven seasons that he played, the highest number of home runs that he had hit in one season was 34. That was far from what the majority of other top homerun hitters have made in their careers. In the beginning of his playing career Bonds was a skilled player. He played his last season for the Pirates in 1992 before looking for opportunities in other clubs.

In 1993, Bonds was signed by in 1993 the San Francisco Giants. The Giants were the first team that Bonds joined. to grow. His first year with the Giants He hit 46 home runs. He also had the batting average at 0.336. There is speculation that he was a user of steroids. As Bonds began to see improvement in his performance, pitchers would often walk Bonds to ensure that they did not give up home runs. On May 28th, 1998 versus the Arizona Diamondbacks, pitcher Gregg Olson was told to deliberately take Barry Bonds out with bases full, instead of attempt to get him out. In the past, no pitcher was able to do exactly what Olson did. It was a blessing for Olson his team, the Diamondbacks were able to prevail the game.

In the years 2000 and 2001, Bonds continued to have incredible home run seasons. Bonds hit 49 home runs in 2000. However, the following year his record was broken for most home runs in one season by hitting 72. He played in his first World Series against their state American League rivals, the Anaheim Angels. The game would be played to the final echelon, however the Giants came up short in the end, falling 4-3.

When Bonds was beginning to close in on the 755-home run record held by Hank Aaron home runs, everybody in baseball started to believe Bonds was going to do whatever required to beat the record. In the final year of his playing career, 2007 Bonds's San Francisco Giants were struggling as did an ageing Bonds was unable to do as much. Bonds only a few home runs away from setting Aaron's record. The season ended with 28 home runs. In August 7, 2007, Bonds broke the record and scored the 756th home run in his career. In the final year of his playing career, Bonds was able to hit 762 career homers. In the present, no athlete has even come even close to breaking the record. Bonds was a final season in San Francisco and retired once the season ended.

8.) 8. Pittsburgh Pirates finishing with a win after 21 years

The Pittsburgh Pirates are not a team you be thinking about when you think of postseasons or championships. Between 1992 and 2013, the Pirates did not just fail to reach the postseason however, they also had an unbeaten record in every season. They have the record for the longest streak of consecutive losses in the entirety of North American professional sports.

In terms of champions winning for Pittsburgh, the capital city of Pittsburgh The Pirates came in at the bottom on the list. There were other Pittsburgh team, the Penguins from the NHL as well as The Steelers in the NFL were winners of numerous championships from 1991 and 2013. Three Stanley Cups for the Penguins and two Super Bowls for the Steelers.

Clint Hurdle was named manager of the Pittsburgh Pirates on November 15th of the Pittsburgh Pirates' manager was named on November 15th. As Hurdle had to work hard to bring back the team which was the worst to lose over the last twenty years but he was able to make changes.

In the month of September 2007, Neal Huntington, the general manager of the Pittsburgh Pirates, hired Dan Fox to develop what was later to turn into MITT (Managing the Information, Tools, and Talent). The software was designed to analyze the places batted balls were struck in games, and determine where the players needed to adjust the field in order to match that batter.

Dan Fox was the new Director of Baseball Systems Development for the Pirates. His program helped to determine the best places for players in the infield should be playing along with shifting times and locations. The Pirates were ranked first for 'out efficiency' 2013. The Pirates players in the infield were awed when they switched towards the right or left in accordance with the batter at hand that they could take that batter out easily. They would usually be delivered directly to the players. It was like they were training to play the game.

Infield shifting was a technique that was not used by the majority of teams however it was the Pirates had the distinction of being among the first team to make it work. The Pirates would, in 2013, be able to win the season having a record of 94 (68) - 94. The Pirates placed 2nd within their National League Central division. They made it into the playoffs at first in their 21-year history and earned the team a wildcard spot.

PitchFX software was a key component. PitchFX software was another important factor in the Pirates' popularity.

PitchFX software tracks the velocity, speed and release points on each pitch that is thrown within the Major Leagues. The Pirates personnel now had software that would determine the pitchers who could throw pitches towards the outer part of the plate and what catchers would convince umpires to declare strikes to their advantage. The program was launched in 2006 and remains useful for every team. When the Pirates had won 94 games during the regular season and then played in the divisional series against the Cardinals and lost to them in just five games.

Droughts can last for a long time or extremely short, however they all happen to us at one point or other. In the sport of sports, when a team is in a drought, it is difficult for fans to support their team, or to help their team. The process of getting out may be the most difficult hurdle to conquer. Also, it helps if there are excellent players in your group. However, often that's not enough. You must also be able to be ready to adjust to changes in the environment when confronted with challenges that are new.

9) Implementation of difficult requests:

Over the course of a century in Major League Baseball, you couldn't get an umpire to alter an order. When the umpire had made the call, that's the end of it. This system of determining calls was detrimental to managers as well as players. For other sports, such as football or basketball coaches can contest the decision of a referee or even overturn it.

The 2nd of June, 2010, Armando Galarraga had a shot in the past to record an all-time winning game against the Detroit Tigers. It was the ninth in the ninth. He was able to retire 26 batters. He wanted to end the game. Jason Donald for his 27th and final pitch. Donald made a catch on an unintentional ground ball that went to the first base.

Galarraga was able to take over first base. Donald was seen to be off in everyone's view, save to Jim Joyce, the first base umpire who afterwards admitted to having did not make the right call. If the call for challenge was in place prior to this time, the official records could have proven that Galarraga had played the game flawlessly. Although this match didn't affect results in any way, an incident like this can cause a lot of damage to the team.

In reality, in game 6, of 1985's World Series, the St. Louis Cardinals were just one far from winning in the World Series against their state adversaries The Kansas City Royals. The base umpire first called the player safe even though he clearly was out of every angle on the replay. Following the blow call and the following hitter made a mistake and landed a blooper on the right field. Two runs were scored, then the Royals won this game, and then game seven to take home their very first World Series.

For the 2014 season, managers were permitted to contest an umpire's decision for each game. There was no difference in whether an umpire did not have the right idea or not, since there was no consequence when an umpire was asked to examine a decision. But, there are some situations that managers aren't able to contest, like strikes and balls.

10.) Jose Altuve and the Houston Astros cheating scandal:

In 2017 in 2017, the Houston Astros won their first World Series against the Los Angeles Dodgers. This was only the second time the Astros participated to play in the World Series. The last time they were in the tournament was in 2005 when they played Chicago White Sox. Chicago White Sox. In 2005, they were part of the National League. They lost the series with a blowout. But the stakes were higher as they were backed by players like Jose Altuve, George Springer and Alex Bregman to back them up. The game lasted seven games. Houston was also scheduled to take part at this year's 2019 World Series, but lost in the World Series to Washington Nationals in seven games.

What was later found out to the League was Houston did not cheat at two of 2017's World Series and the 2019 World Series. A YouTuber with the username "JomboyMedia," and which is also known by the name of Jimmy O'Brien, discovered that the 2019 Astros included a camera the place that relayed signals to the batters that came into the game. Additionally, he discovered that the

Astros were transmitting signals to batters using trash bins. The result was that players to use the Astros batters to receive better pitches to their advantage. The Astros have created a system in which one player would hit on a trash container if it was a changeup or curveball. It would not bang in the case of a fastball or slider and the batter was to act in accordance with these signals in order to benefit themselves.

Following the discovery that the Astros were cheating in the year 2019 after the 2019 World Series, the MLB examined the team's 2017. World Series win and discovered that they'd committed similar things. In the year 2018 Alex Cora went to the Boston Red Sox as the manager. He was able to win the World Series with them. There was speculation that the team employed an alarm system to beat the Dodgers to secure the World Series in five games. The MLB is now publishing records books that contain asterisks in order in order to alert people that the Astros were cheating during 2017. World Series.

In the 2017 postseason it was possible to allow to the New York Yankees to play in the World Series against the Dodgers. The Yankees will never be able to tell what could have transpired if they had not been swindled. All we have is the fact that they took the fans of a fair World Series. The sports scandal is thought to be among the most infamous of the 21st century, and maybe in all baseball. The culprit was Jose Altuve however, not just did he collaborate with his teammates to bribe the Yankees as well as the Dodgers and the Dodgers, but it has also led to Aaron Judge losing an MVP award.

11) 11) Washington Nationals winning the 2019 World Series:

Washington D.C. is typically not thought of as an area that is a champion sports city. There were only two championship teams in the city. Washington Bullets and the Washington Redskins were the only team that won a championship following the Senators quit for Arlington, Texas. In the end, however, the Washington Bullets, now referred to as the Wizards have won only one title in the 1977-78 seasons. The Redskins however, in contrast were able to win three Super Bowl Championships in 1982 1993, 1987 and 1991. There were two more championships prior to that Super Bowl era in 1937 and 1942. In the absence of any titles, it appeared that D.C. would never get another championship. But, that was to change in the year 2018 as it was the year that Washington Capitals won their first Stanley Cup.

The Montreal Expos were relocated to Montreal into Washington D. C. in order to be known as the Washington Nationals for the 2005 MLB season. The team was not great during their early seasons, yet nobody thought that they'd become the World Series team. The season of 2019 started off with a rocky beginning for the Nationals having an overall record of 19-31. Every person who watched baseball living in Washington believed that the team would be among the most disappointing teams in the National League by the end of the season. Then, slowly but surely, the perception started to shift. The Nationals were beginning to turn things around. At the close their season they had made the second-place finish as well as a wildcard spot having an average of 93 - the Nationals had a record of 69.

When the playoffs rolled around when the playoffs began, the Nationals defeated their Milwaukee Brewers 3 - 2 in the Wild Card game to make it into the playoff round for divisional teams.

When they entered the divisional series, they were to take on their opponents, the Los Angeles Dodgers. They were the Dodgers which had the most impressive record in major leagues having an average of 106-56, and were viewed as winners of in the World Series. The Nationals beat the Dodgers by five games three-to-two during the game. When the Nationals beat the Dodgers in that series, individuals began to believe they had the chance to win everything.

The second team they had to face were the St. Louis Cardinals. They smashed their way to their National League pennant, by beating the Cardinals 4-1.

The American League, the Houston Astros beat their rivals the New York Yankees for the second time in three seasons in order to claim the pennant. They Houston Astros were favored to be victorious in their first World Series. It seemed like everything was going very well during the Nationals in the beginning. They scored a 2 - 1 in the Series defeating them by beating the Astros on Minute Maid Park. When the Series came back to D. C., the Astros beat the Nationals in every game, they led the series by 3 to 2. In the final game at Minute Maid Park, the Nationals were able to win game six. In the end, the Series was tied in game 7 played at Minute Maid Park.

Game 7 began with a win for the Astros with the Astros going ahead 1-1 in the second innings. The Astros got one more hit in the bottom of the 5th with the help of an RBI single. Near the end of the game's seventh innings The Nationals were on the right track and took the lead by scoring the home run of Anthony Rendon as well as a home run of two runs by Howie Kendrick, giving the Nationals a three-to-two advantage. Daniel Hudson struck out the last batter and the Nationals were victorious in game seven by a score of 6 2. The World Series is the only postseason game that has been played in any sport that no team was able to win an at-home game.

12) 12. MLB will be coming to London:

The UK is likely to be the only country that you could imagine hosting the next MLB game. In 2019 it was the case that

Boston Red Sox and New York Yankees were set to play one the other in a classic two-game rivalry game. The game took place at London Stadium in London, United Kingdom. Setting up the stadium was an issue. The baseball stadium was not there to be found in London. They converted the typical football or soccer arena into a baseball field. Like the typical double-use stadiums, this one was designed for baseball and football. they put fans from the excitement.

The Yankees were victorious in each game. They took the opening game 17-13, while the game that followed was 12-8.

13.) Billy Bean and the Los Angeles A's win streak of 20 consecutive games:

It was the Money Ball system implemented by Billy Bean was the most innovative analytical method employed in the field of sports. Through the analysis of a batter's OBP as well as OBPS, they could identify the hidden talent of a player and then put them in the starting lineup. The 2003 Oakland Athletics struggled to win matches, however after the program was put into place, the Athletics started to show off.

Following the Carlos Pena trade to the Detroit Tigers, Scott Hatterberg began his first season as the primary first baseman of the Athletics. Because of his high in-base rate and his improved on-base percentage, the A's started to enjoy a winning streak.

Following their series sweeps on the road after their road series sweeps, the A's were back at home in hopes of achieving a the longest winning streak in 20 games. The Athletics were playing against the Kansas City Royals. The Athletics were ahead 11-0 in the initial three innings but once the fourth innings arrived, the game began to shift. The fourth inning's top revealed the weaknesses of the A's, since they conceded five runs against the Royals. The Royals were able to get back on track. In the middle nineth of ninth, it looked that the chance of winning 20 games was about to come to an end. As the game was locked at 11-11 The A's stand the chance of beating the Royals in the final game of ninth. Scott Hatterberg came to the plate in the role of pinch-hitter in the hope of getting himself on the base. However, when he spotted speedy balls right above the plate, he hit it and drove it the deep right field to score an individual walk-off homer.

Oakland reached the playoffs in that year, but was defeated by Minnesota's Minnesota Twins in the division series by 3 games to 2. Even although the Athletics were not able to win all the games however, they showed the rest of baseball there is no one person who creates a winning team It's the mix of players who bring their abilities in a team.

14) 14) The 2001 World Series and the ending of a dynasty

The New York Yankees dynasty was unique in the world of professional sports in the 1990s through 2000. In 2000, the New York Yankees would face the Arizona Diamondbacks in the 2001 World Series. This, the 2001 World Series, was the first World Series after 9/11. It was also an historic World Series for the Diamondbacks because they were only the second expansion team to take home an award in the early years.

The Yankees hope to take home their first World Series title one more time in

New York, appeared to be in a good position to repeat the feat. This could be a World Series that would go all the way to the finish line.

It was clear that the 2001 World Series was a pitching contest. Stars such as Randy Johnson and Curt Schilling The Diamondbacks could stifle the Yankees players. Additionally, thanks to stars like Luis Gonzalez, they were capable of keeping pace against the Yankees.

The Yankees began the game losing 2-0 in the game. Game 3 did have their side winning, due to the assistance of Roger Clemens and Mariano Rivera The Yankees managed to pull out a victory against the Diamondbacks in their home. Game 4 will require additional innings, however the Yankees had a chance to prevail against the Diamondbacks thanks to the single home run at the final tenth by Derek Jeter.

Game 5 took place playing in New York. The series was tied at two-to-two, it was now anybody's World Series to claim. The Yankees defeated the Red Sox in game 5, with a scores of 3 - 2 over twelve innings.

Game 6 will provide the Diamondbacks an opportunity to win. The Diamondbacks won 15-2. Game 7 looked only for the Yankees however, when the game reached the end of the ninth, things began to change. Mariano Rivera was brought into the game in the 8th innings and the Manager Joe Torre and kept him there for the 9th. The Diamondbacks made use of Rivera when they noticed that he was struggling. After Jay Bell getting aboard and the Diamondbacks tied the game at 2-2, Luis

Gonzalez came to the plate with the bases stacked, and struck an easy blooper to deep center field, winning game 7 with three to 2. It is the very only World Series that the Yankees had lost since. The Yankees' dynasty had ended.

15) The 1994 strike:

The 1990s were a time when Major League Baseball was all the popular. Baseball movies were released frequently and TV viewers at record levels, there seemed to be no barrier that could hinder the MLB from taking off to new heights.

The NBA as well as the NFL were the first professional leagues in history to introduce salary caps. MLB owners initially believed this could be advantageous to the MLB. Bud Selig and the owners of the Major League teams, proposed certain changes regarding how players will receive compensation. These included a strict wage cap and no arbitration of salary, more efficient timetables for free agents the benefits of players based on income, a licensing revenue split between owners and players, as well as the revenue share of players was decreased to 50 percent. From the standpoint of the player, this arrangement is a nightmare. The association of players would not be able to comply with the terms of this agreement.

On the 12th of August 1994, a strike was initiated. The strike caused being canceled the rest of the season, including the playoffs and the World Series, a potential 0.400 annual batting average for Tony Gwynn and possibly that of the Montreal Expos winning the World Series.

The strike of the players focused on the salary cap proposed by the MLBPA was not keen on. While this was a rule within the NBA as well as the NFL but the MLB had a different structure. One reason was that players were accustomed to earning their own money as well as being able to make the majority of their decisions. In 1994, the World Series is only the second World Series canceled in MLB history.

Chapter 10: What Is Baseball?

Baseballs thrown on surface of the baseball field.

America has the credit of creating a variety of sports, including basketball, baseball and gridiron football to mention a few. Baseball however, is perhaps the most well-known of these creations. Since the time of the Civil War, it has been called the "American game', even as it gains popularity throughout Latin American and Asian countries throughout the world.

The game of baseball is played using a bat small round ball as well as the glove. There are nine spots on the field to defend which requires all players to use gloves to capture the ball. Batters are also required to wear helmets in order for protection of their head as they confront the Pitcher. Likewise, the person who plays the role of a Catcher in the middle of the field, sports an arm plate with a helmet, a mask for the face with shin protectors, knee protectors.

In terms of offense, each team is equipped with a lengthy bat that is usually constructed of aluminum or wood. The batter is trying to knock the ball away from the range of team members who are wearing gloves in the field. After the ball has been hit, the ball is thrown across the field in a diamond shape and crosses the bases in their course. Four bases are available including the fourth, Home Plate.

If a player crosses the three bases before them and makes it Home the player earns one point. A player can pause at any point but do not need to cover all three bases simultaneously.

If the player makes it all through to Home with just one strike this is referred to as the Home Run. Another approach to achieving an Home Run is to hit the ball beyond the park. This means that the ball has been hit over the boundaries of the field, where the defense can't take control over the ball. The team with the greatest number of runs (points) at the conclusion of 9 innings (times at bat) takes the lead in the game.

To defend, gloves are used to try and take the ball that is hit by the batter. If a batter is hit before they reach the ground, they will be removed from the field. When a fielder is able to catch the ball up on the ground before it ever touches the ground, this is considered to be a way of getting out. Another option to gain an out is to force out.

If a batter has to run towards a base but has no alternative to get back to the base that was previously used, the fielder is able to contact the base with the ball rather than tagging the player to count as an out. Force outs occur when a batter runs towards First Base, or when the runner is accompanied by another who is on the base to their left.

Also when a runner is sitting on First Base and the ball is struck by the batter, then there's an out force for both First as well as Second Base. Another method of getting an exemption for the defense is to rely on the pitcher. When the Pitcher throws balls which land within the predetermined space, known as the strike zone, and the batter is unable to hit the ball 3 times during a single game this is referred to as a strike. Defense must score three strikes, using one of the methods mentioned earlier prior to their team have a shot to bat.

Baseball Fielding Positions

There are nine positions for fielding in baseball. The job of the fielder is to make the required three outs in order to bat with their team. Nine positions:

1. Pitcher

2. Catcher

3. First Base

4. Second Base

5. Third Base

6. Shortstop

7. Right Field

8. Centerfield

9. Left Field

In addition, the baseball field is split into two parts: the Infield as well as the Outfield. The positions are spread across the field. This is an image of a baseball court for you to get a better picture of what I'm speaking about.

The Infield

The Infield comprises the first six positions that are listed in the previous paragraphs. They are situated on the dirt covered portion of the diamond-shaped field. Infield players Infield have to throw with a high ability. The job of the Infield players is to mark out runners in order to prevent opponents from making runs.

The goal of players playing in Infield Infield is to prevent the ball from escaping their line of sight into the Outfield ahead of their backs. They have to play with precision the balls that are thrown at them, and ensure that the ball is under their own hands. The runners are less chances to get around the bases to get the distance to Home Plate, and also allows them to get out of the way much easier.

The Pitcher

The pitcher is accountable for pitching the ball to the batter. They're located at the center of the Infield and are situated on the top of a tiny and elevated hill known as "the mound of the pitcher. It is also common to hear players call it "the mound" or "the hill. Each game starts by the Pitcher. The Pitcher is seated on the mound, which is located in the center of the field that is shaped like a diamond. They have to throw the ball across the strike zone at which point the batter is given the opportunity to strike it and swing. Strike zone refers to the space between the knees and shoulders for batters and is within the limits of Home Plate. If the batter fails to hit there is struck. Three strikes indicate that the batter is out and is counted as one of the three outs that the defense must get for the offense to take over.

If the Pitcher fails to put the ball in the strike zone, and the batter is not swinging at it, then the pitch is known as an "ball. It is generally accepted that the batter should not strike the ball as it's not within the designated area. If the pitcher has four balls toss and the batter is given the opportunity to play First Base and not be removed by the fielders.

After batters make it to the base, another task of the Pitchers is to stop the player from moving. In baseball, a runner may try to steal a base. A pitcher must be on guard for the player and then throw the ball towards the fielder who is in charge to try to catch the runner. If successful the ball is counted as one of three outs that are required. If this occurs this is referred to as an out by the Pitcher.

Pitchers throw different types of pitches in varying speeds. The pitches that are most commonly used are: fastball slider, curveball changing-up, knuckleball, and change-up.

One of the most well-known is the speedball. A few of the top Pitchers are able to throw the ball for over 100 mph (Baseball Positions, 2020). One that is the hardest pitches to throw is a curveball which is also difficult to hit in the right way, when thrown. It is due to the fact that once the Pitcher has successfully used this type of pitch, it starts to curve towards the batter in the end of the game. The batter may be fooled by the motion of the ball. They may fail to see the ball. Take into consideration all the things that a batter should be aware of while playing! The ball is flying at them at speeds of up to 90 miles an hour, and they must determine if the ball is within the strike zone. when they swing, does it swerve away in the final seconds ... this is quite a lot of things to consider within a short period of time!

When a ball is delivered to a Pitcher game is then stopped. There is no way for runners to proceed on to the next position after the game has ended.

Pitchers should be cautious. They may suffer shoulder injuries due to the prolonged usage of their arm. The shoulder injuries can be severe and hard to recover from. In the event of serious injuries, they can cause the loss of the season for Pitchers, or sometimes, even the end of their career.

To protect their arms, pitchers need to "warm up" prior to entering in the game. When playing professional baseball, you are likely to observe Pitchers warming up alongside their pitching coach or teammate or even the catcher. It's easy to warm up throwing the ball around along with another person, throwing the ball harder and faster every time. Then they'll stretch to loosen their muscles. The warm-up is usually done in a place known as a bullpen. It's tiny space on the left of the field that is separated from players. If you play the case of recreational baseball, you'll probably see Pitchers warming up along with Catchers in the middle of the field prior to when the batter gets his spot.

Everyone should perform an appropriate warm-up prior to playing, however this is especially crucial for the pitcher.

The Catcher

The job of the catcher is to crawl in front of Home Plate and catch the pitch thrown at them by Pitcher. The catcher can be found on the other side of the field from the mound of the Pitcher, and facing the Pitcher. If the batter fails to hit or the ball gets placed outside of the zone of the strike, the Catcher has to stop the movement of the ball in order to stop runners from taking bases. Similar to the Pitcher, the Catcher may also throw the ball over others fielders in order to catch the runners. The Catcher also has the responsibility to guard Home Plate when the runners attempt to score. Fielders are able to throw balls to the catcher in order to knock the runner and stop the runner from scoring points.

The Catcher should also maintain an excellent connection with the Pitcher in the event that they can tell what pitches will be thrown. It is essential that the player knows which pitch is being throwing to to correctly catch it. Sometimes, the coach and manager may signal the Catcher on which pitch to throw. Then, the catcher is then able to indicate to the Pitcher. Signals are employed to stop the batter unaware of what pitch is being pitched. If the batter did be aware, it would give the defense an unfair advantage the defense.

Sometimes Pitchers decide on his own pitch, and the Catcher will use signals to determine which they would like to choose. The pitcher shakes his head, or nod in agreement when they are asked, to ensure that they're both ready for the type of pitch that will be thrown. Each team uses distinct signals for various pitches. In the past they were caught, Houston Astros Houston Astros were caught in an investigation into cheating in which they tried to steal pitches from teams in order to gain an advantage.

The position of the Catcher is usually thought to be among the toughest position in baseball to perform. They're the only defensive position player that is able to see the whole field from the point of view that of a batter. Also, they have to maintain a the position of crouching for long periods of duration, and wear the most robust protective gear. They must crouch in front of the batter. The gear they are wearing is vital for safety of the Catcher because the ball or bat could hit the player and inflict injury.

A catcher with all of his gear.

First Baseman

The First Baseman has the responsibility of protecting the base to which batters can run following hitting the ball. They're located behind the Catcher. They are also just behind and to the left side of Pitcher. After a ball has been hit, the fielders will throw the ball towards the First

Baseman, so that they may identify the runner. First Baseman may either tag the base or player for the out.

First Baseman can be a very difficult post. The ball is thrown at them frequently since every play involves an individual batter who is running towards First which means they're responsible for making sure they be able to catch the ball each time. If they do not get the ball to them that is thrown to them, they give the runner the chance to skip First Base and keep running towards Next Base. First Baseman get the most of the action in the game, aside from the Catcher and Pitcher. It is the case that there's always a lot of force to be at First Base, because the batter has to be there prior to moving. Although, no matter how often the ball is hit to First however, it is not often hit directly at this player as most batters are left-handed. Also, they must have the ability to throw with a good arm. be capable of throwing the ball over the field towards the Third Baseman or The Catcher.

Second Baseman

The Second Baseman is the guard of Second Base. They're positioned in front of the Pitcher with the back. They typically stand somewhere between First Base and Second Base. In this position, the player has to be swift to their feet and prepared to play a ball on any moment. The field is usually that the ball will be hitting, and they are required be quick to get it into First Base for the ball to the field. Second Basemen are also able to catch highest number of double plays, where two players are separated in the same game.

Second Basemen must also be a backup for the Pitcher. If the catcher is throwing the ball back there's a possibility that it will be missed by the Pitcher. catch. Second Basemen must be on hand to take the ball so that runners are prevented from getting bases stolen when the ball isn't in the control of the ball.

And lastly, Second Base is the base where runners typically attempt to steal every time they have the opportunity. It's more difficult for a Catcher to prevent Second Base stealing then it is Third Base because of how long they need to throw their ball. Furthermore, as it's in the middle of the Pitcher, it's impossible for the Pitcher to see when a runner attempts to take Second. Also, they have the highest Force outs after the first baseman.

Third Baseman

The Third Baseman protects Third Base. They're positioned on the left side of the Catcher. They are between and just to the left from the Pitcher. The majority of batters attempt to strike balls in toward Third Base, as this will allow the player more time to reach First Base before they can be penalized. The majority of balls also are targeted this way as a result of the large number of batters who are right handed. The Third Baseman should have a powerful throwing arm in order to leap across the field First Base. Third Base is the last base to go before Home Plate, so the Third Baseman should be cautious not to allow anyone through their position.

As with the Second Baseman Third Baseman also has to be swift on their feet. The area around Third Base is known as "the hot corner" because a lot of balls hitting this region leave the bat swiftly and forcefully. It is their responsibility to take the ball in their hands and to throw it back to First Base, as well as safeguard their base or the player who is trying to access the base. They're also the last first line of defense prior to Home Plate and the Catcher They are also under lots of pressure to keep runners off their feet.

Shortstop

Shortstops are located between Third and Second Base between the two bases, in the direction to the left of Pitcher. The job of the Shortstop is to protect Second base when the Second Baseman is playing with the ball. Additionally, they play the role of a 'cutoff man' to the outfielders when the ball has been over the mentioned players. When the ball goes in the grass and the Shortstop has to go to the grass in order for the outfielders (usually Left or Centerfield) to throw the ball. The Shortstop will then throw the ball either to Second and Third Base, allowing them to take out players. The Shortstops are situated on the same hot corner therefore they will have plenty to accomplish during a game.

Shortstops also have the responsibility of blocking runners that are who are trying to take Second as well as Third Base. They assist the Second Baseman whenever they are tasked with throwing the ball onto them at the field.

It's also crucial to shortstops Shortstop to be fast and athletic. They must be able to catch the ball whenever it is thrown to them and also have the strength in throwing it out of the Outfield while they serve as the cutoff guy.

The Outfield

The players are who are standing on the Outfield

The Outfield includes three players that are: Right Fielder, Centre Fielder and Left Fielder. They're located within the grass, just outside the diamond-shaped shape of the Infield. They are the ones that catch the highest number of flying balls (balls which are suspended in the air prior to when they land on the ground, meaning an instant release).

In the Outfield require extremely powerful throwing arms as well as excellent ability to read the ball. If a ball gets completely to them, they must catch the ball. This is one of the main things they must do. Another important aspect is throwing the ball back towards the field in case any the other runners require to be removed from the field. Most of the time, they serve as the final first line of defense against the possibility of a Home Run.

Right Fielder

Right Fielders can be found on the Outfield just behind the first baseman. In addition to getting the ball caught and returning it to the Infield The Right Fielders are expected to be a backup for with the player who is first. After the ball has been delivered towards the First Baseman the Right Fielder needs to be right behind them so that they can catch any balls missed, and then regain control over the game. The result is lower bases taken and less runs being scored.

As with the First Basemen Right Fielders must have strong throwing arms. They must take on a large amount of space within the Outfield and should be in a position to throw the ball into third. Since the majority of batters are left-handed, Right Field is where the most balls get struck. But, if the left-handed batsman is set to bat, the right fielder must be prepared for any situation since any ball that is hit for a long distance will go towards right field.

Center Fielder

Center Fielders sit on the center of the Outfield on the grass right to the left of Second Base. The Center Fielders lead the group of players within the Outfield. Each time a fly ball is thrown into the Outfield and players do not know who should take it The Center Fielder is in charge of catching the ball or signalling the ball to the Left or Right Fielder to take. It is vital because when players are gazing up to the sky to see the ball they could risk colliding with each other, which could result in injuries.

The Center Fielder is one of the most fast players in the team. There is a lot of terrain to be covering on the Outfield and must be fast enough to cover the ground. A lot of Home Runs are achieved by throwing the ball directly into the center field which is why the player who is who is in the position needs to be able to catch the ball rapidly and return the ball to the Infield (usually the Shortstop if the ball is sunk in the turf). If the ball hits on top of their head it is essential that they are quick enough to catch the ball, as well as robust enough to throw the ball back into the Infield.

Left Fielder

The Left Fielder can be found between the grass and Third Base, typically settled between the Third Baseman and Shortstop. They are in the same spot as previously mentioned infielders. The majority of baseballs are hit in Left Field because so many batters are left-handed.

Left Fielders are among the very few athletes who aren't required to have a powerful throwing arm. They are rarely required to throw the ball to First Base, usually only throwing the ball towards Third Base or to the Shortstop. If the ball hits the left fielder's head the Shortstop will follow them to the grass, reducing the distance that the Left Fielder is required to make the throw.

The Batter

While the batter's position isn't physically a role like those mentioned earlier however, it's still a topic to consider. Batters perform an essential job that is to make a score. The ability to hit a small ball towards you at 100 miles per hour isn't a small task as well, and neither does it hit far enough and swift enough to stop players from being able to catch the ball.

Batters play their positions between the Pitcher and Catcher. If they're left-handed they'll be to the right from Home Plate, the left of the player. The hand they are most dominantly directed towards the Catcher as the force of their strike comes from dragging the bat across Home Plate so that it hits the ball. Left-handed players are on the opposite part of the plate and their right hand is facing towards the Pitcher.

As the ball travels across the strike zone the batter begins their swing. The bat is lengthy, thinner toward where it grips (where the batter grips the bat) but large and round toward the top. The batter would like the ball to strike the middle of the bat or else they could injure their hands. This also gives you greater power and a more powerful hitting.

If the batter strikes their ball with a bat, they release the bat before to run: do not to throw the bat instead, let it go. If the batter is caught throwing the bat on their shoulders prior to running it could be ruled out by the umpire as a result of the potential danger that the bat could cause. The majority of batters let the bat fall out of their fingers after they have swung it which is why it falls safely into the earth behind them.

The runners must run toward First and wait for their coach - or in some situations, their teammate to to stop at First or proceed towards Second. The coach or the player will be close to Third and can instruct the runner to take a break at the Second, or continue towards Third (they are also accountable for informing the runner that they should not stop at Third, or to go on towards Home Plate). They must be aware of the ball closely and inform their players whether the ball is under control of fielders or not. This way, runners can be focused on his running, not trying to locate the ball on the field.

If a batter waits for their turn, they typically are positioned in a specific zone on the field within the foul zone. There are many who call the batter being"on deck. Once a batter is finished after his turn may move to a base (if the hit was good) or go back into the dugout (if they were struck out) that is where the players are seated when they're not on the field. If they strike the ball, and then go to an area, they must take the bat away from Home Plate. Most of the time, the batter following will pick up the bat, and then toss it (carefully) back into the dugout, where it will be cleared aside. When playing in the Major Leagues, an employee on behalf of the team would typically take the bat in place of the batter who is next.

Bases

A photo of a base in an open field.

Before getting into the baseball rules and the rules of baseball, let's be talking about bases. As I mentioned earlier, the players do not need to cover all bases within a single swing. It is possible to have multiple runners at base simultaneously. It is possible to have a runner on Second and First or Third and so on. When there are three bases that are hosting runners the situation is termed as bases filled. This can mean a variety of things to the defense.

The first is that every base comes with an option to force out, which includes Home Plate. The catcher has to be prepared to help an errant runner, thereby preventing scoring a point. In addition, runners on Third Base runs the risk that the runner will try to rob Home Plate (though this is rare within Major League Baseball, MLB).

The Pitcher, in turn, must be under great pressure to stop the batter from taking a hit, and to keep his team members home. The Pitcher should also make certain not to throw the four balls needed to walk the batter onto First in order to let the offense be successful and keeps the bases full.

Third is the only base that could be taken. There are rare occasions when there may be a runner trying to steal

Home from Third. However, this is extremely rare within the Major Leagues.

Then, when the bases are full when a batter hits the ball with a Home Run, it means four points for the offensive. This is known as the Grand Slam, and it rarely happens within the Major Leagues. It is possible to hear about what's known as a ground roll double. The term refers to a situation where the batter is hit by the ball outside of the park, however it touches the ground prior to that (usually the ball rolls under fences). Instead of being counted as an Home Run it is given a double, and is then moved into Second Base.

For batters, there's a ton of terminology about the bases. When you see people say that a batter is hitting a single indicates that they were able to reach First after hitting the ball however, they needed to put it down. Double indicates they reached the Second position, while a triple indicates they made it up to Third.

Finally, you'll see many players get filthy in the course of play. If they are running towards the base, or even stealing it players often attempt to slide so as to prevent getting tagged by fielders. The runner slides down to the ground and plunges to the base whether head or feet first. It is the most popular form of sliding in Home Plate, but can occur anywhere.

A runner slides into the base while other players tag him.

Once you've mastered the fundamentals of every position, as well as how important bases are and the various lingo we can discuss the rules of baseball as well as the proper way to play.

Rules of Baseball

Baseball rules differ. It takes time to learn them. There are umpires present throughout the game to make sure that the rules are adhered to. Umpires make the decision on whether a pitcher threw strikes or not. they determine if the runner has been caught out, or did safe to return safely to base. They also decide if a ball was hitting into fair or foul area. They also are responsible for making sure that the ball's size can play the right way for the match. When playing in the Major Leagues, the life duration of a ball is between five and seven innings. The umpire has the responsibility of taking the ball off (if it's not been handed to a person or kicked from the park) and then giving the pitcher a brand new ball.

Fair territory refers to the space that lies between the lines around the perimeter of the field. Every ball that is that falls within these lines is considered fair and thus being played. The balls hit beyond these boundaries are considered to be foul which count as strikes against a batter even though they do not be counted as the third strike. When playing in the Major Leagues, many fans collect and save the balls for souvenirs. They can be later offered for sale at a fair value, contingent upon the player. A ball, for instance, struck by Babe Ruth can earn a collector quite a bit of cash.

It must have at least nine players on an entire team to participate (most professional teams include many more). If the team is not able to field nine players, it must be forced to forfeit the game. The positions on the field have to be filled to take part in the game.

The game lasts for minimum nine innings each giving each team a opportunity to bat and make runs. When the teams are tied after nine innings, additional innings are played in order to make the tie break. The home team (the team that is on the field that which the match is played on) is always the one to take to the pitch first. Another team, referred to as the guest, is allowed to bat first. The term "inning" is often described by the top and bottom that means the beginning or second portion of the innings.

Also, if you hear someone saying "it's the top of the fifth," this indicates that the opposing team is playing at the opening of the fifth innings. In contrast the time someone mentions that"it's in the "bottom of eighth," this means that the home team will be playing at the conclusion of the eighth innings.

What, then, to remember these regulations? The simplest way to remember them is to break them into smaller pieces.

Batting Rules

Batting players must play according to a specific order that is set prior to the start each game. When a batting sequence is set, it can't be altered. But, coaches are able to substitute players in the order of batting, however the replacement must be at the same position that the person they replace. The person who fills in the place of the batter is called an "in-between" batter. It is usually done in order to make a more competent hitter in the place of a player who has different skills. As an example, Pitchers tend to be weak in batting, and so could have a pinch hitter to hit their needs.

The batter is given three strikes prior to being out. If the umpire declares the pitch strikes, it's considered to be a strike even if they don't strike the pitch. If they miss a swing an opportunity, they are considered to be an unintentional strike, whether within striking zone it is not. If the ball is thrown to the foul zone and miss, they are not able the chance to move into First Base. If it bounces off of the bat, and then goes over the batter, it's known as a foul tip, and could count as the second and first strike just as any other foul ball.

When a batter is struck through the ball that is to be thrown by the Pitcher the batter gets the right to a base, as long as they do not suffer any injuries. It means that the batter can stroll to First Base without the threat of being struck out. If a batter is not able to stay in the field because of an injury or pain, a different player will take their place at the base and run around the field. The manager is responsible of deciding which runner will replace the base that of the batter.

The batter is waiting to get his chance.

Fielding Rules

Pitchers attempt to hit strikes that are too quick or complicated for batters. The goal is to hit all batters, without needing to catch all balls. If they achieve this it is referred to as shut out, also known as the no-hitter.

In the event that a ball gets hit onto the field, players try to catch it in the air. If this occurs the ball is classified as to be a fly ball. If they are able to catch it prior to it touching the ground in fair terrain, this count as one out. The teams need three outs to allow the teams to shift between defense and offense.

If the ball hits the ground, it's described as a groundball. The fielders must crawl down and hold the ball with their hands. Then, they must tag runners, mark their bases, or throw the ball to the appropriate person to complete the mission. The ball being thrown to the ground doesn't count as a strike, therefore runners must be identified for the chance to get at least one of those three points.

A fielder gets ready to receive a ball from the ground.

Balls that are hit in the foul zone are removed and the pitcher gets another ball to pitch to the batter. It is not possible to score runs by an infected ball.

Uniform Rules

A good example of how is a baseball cap.

As per the National Federation of State Highschool Associations The uniforms for one team must have the same color and look. The uniforms consist of shirts or the jersey, caps, pants, as well as shoes. But, if a player is wearing protective headwear (such as helmets) it will substitute for the head hat. It is mandatory to wear a helmet while players bat. Catchers must also wear helmets when they're playing (Baseball Uniform Rules, 2016,)

Each sleeve's length for the individual players must be the same length. The sleeves must not be ripped or torn. If a person wears lengthy sleeves underneath their shirt, they should be black or a darker color. Pitchers cannot wear anything that is on their hand or arm which could distract the batter. The uniforms must not have unsafe buttons or reflective accessories. Every player should be wearing their own number on the reverse of their shirt.

www.ingramcontent.com/pod-product-compliance
Lightning Source LLC
Chambersburg PA
CBHW071439080526
44587CB00014B/1918